Jacob Dolson Cox

**The second Battle of Bull Run**

Jacob Dolson Cox

**The second Battle of Bull Run**

ISBN/EAN: 9783743328204

Manufactured in Europe, USA, Canada, Australia, Japa

Cover: Foto ©Andreas Hilbeck / pixelio.de

Manufactured and distributed by brebook publishing software (www.brebook.com)

Jacob Dolson Cox

**The second Battle of Bull Run**

# THE
## SECOND BATTLE
### OF
# BULL RUN,

AS CONNECTED WITH THE

## FITZ-JOHN PORTER CASE.

A Paper read before the Society of Ex-Army and Navy Officers of Cincinnati, February 28, 1882.

BY

## JACOB D. COX,
*Late Maj. Gen. Commanding 23d Army Corps.*

---

CINCINNATI:
PETER G. THOMSON,
1882.

# PREFACE.

In the following paper my aim has been to bring together the evidence bearing on a few decisive points. Whoever settles these solidly in his mind will find a trustworthy clue to the intricacies of the great mass of testimony in the three bulky volumes which make up the Congressional documents relating to the case. To comment upon all the varying statements of witnesses, and formally weigh all the discrepancies, would itself require a volume. For those who may have the leisure for it, it would be interesting; but the judgment will turn, at last, upon the way one looks at the few central points. The question is whether an officer did his duty in a given situation. To answer it, we have to know what his orders were, and whether he obeyed them. If he did not, we have to inquire what means he took to discover the condition of affairs on the field, and what zeal and energy he showed in efforts to do this and to carry out his instructions. His conduct must be judged in the light of what he knew, and the spirit he showed.

Facts which he did not know, and took no proper military means to discover, can not favorably affect the character of his conduct. The conclusion reached, however, is that the more of the facts we know, the worse the conduct appears. It will be better for the dignity of the country that a former judgment of a court should not be reversed on grounds that will not bear the ultimate test of historical scrutiny. To help form a right judgment now, is the motive for consenting to the publication of a paper, the preparation of which is sufficiently explained in its opening paragraphs.

In the appendix will be found the substance of most of the evidence which has been distinctly referred to in the text, both documentary and oral. It is but a small part of the whole, but it will enable those who have not access to the complete report, to see the character and logical connection of facts which must be wholly ignored or overborne before one can reach the conclusions which General Porter asks us to accept.

# TABLE OF CONTENTS.

|     |     |     |
| --- | --- | --- |
| I. | Introductory | 1 |
| II. | March from Warrenton Junction | 8 |
| III. | Discrepancies in Testimony | 14 |
| IV. | Time of Longstreet's arrival | 16 |
| V. | Schenck's and Reynolds' movements | 20 |
| VI. | Errors in Recollection | 28 |
| VII. | Longstreet's position on the field | 30 |
| VIII. | Map of the Battlefield | 31 |
| IX. | Porter's conduct | 50 |
| X. | The Half-past-four order | 62 |
| XI. | Porter's dispatches | 64 |
| XII. | Appendix . | |
| | 1. Porter's letters to Burnside | 73 |
| | 2. Pope's orders to Porter | 76 |
| | 3. Porter's dispatches to McDowell | 79 |
| | 4. Dispatches of other officers | 81 |
| | 5. Official reports, National officers, | 85 |
| | 6. Official reports, Confederate officers | 86 |
| | 7. Oral testimony | 93 |
| | 8. General Garfield's opinion in 1880 | 119 |
| XIII. | Index | 121 |

# THE
# SECOND BATTLE OF BULL RUN.

GENTLEMEN OF THE SOCIETY. — Although my judgment concerning the case of General Fitz-John Porter was sharply defined, and my belief was strong that the so-called newly-discovered evidence in itself tended rather to confirm the judgment of the Court-martial which condemned him, than to make any good ground for the reversal of the sentence and the bestowal of honors and emoluments, which was recommended by the recent Board of Investigation, I still was unwilling to take part in the public discussion of the matter. My reasons were chiefly personal ones, based on old friendships and associations, and would have controlled me but for the circumstances which made public my letter on the subject to General Garfield, without my consent.

The letter was written in February, 1880, when General Garfield had no expectation of being made a candidate for the Presidency, but was preparing himself to defend, in the House of Representatives, the judgment of the Court-martial of which he was a member. Not long afterward he had casually allowed a common acquaintance of himself and General Porter to read the letter, and Porter thus became acquainted with an outline of its contents. On the 24th of May, of the same year, General Porter wrote to me, telling me of his partial knowledge of the letter, and asking for a copy of it, that he might give me proofs of the errors into which I had fallen, and enable me to correct them.

Naturally surprised at this, I demurred to what seemed to be opening the door to a controversy with one in his unhappy situation. On referring the request to General Garfield, he consented to my acceding to General Porter's wish, and I did so. Meanwhile, the Convention at Chicago met, and the wonderful series of events, beginning with Garfield's nomination and election, and ending with his murder, followed. I mention the dates given above, that it may be clearly seen that the correspondence, Porter's request for a copy, and Garfield's consent, had nothing whatever to do with the Presidential canvass, with which, I have been told, there has been some attempt to associate Garfield's attitude to the case.

Somewhat later I learned that copies of my letter were in the hands of members of the Board; that General Porter had printed a reply to it; and that whether I would or no, I was driven from the attitude of private criticism into one of public debate. Happily, the friendships which had made me wish to avoid discussion were too well-founded to be affected by differences of opinion. When, therefore, I learned that this Society desired to have a somewhat fuller presentation of my views, I no longer saw any good reason for hesitating to speak on the subject.

In December, 1862, a Court-martial tried General Porter upon charges and specifications duly preferred, on which he was arraigned for criminal insubordination and disobedience of orders upon the battle-field. The Court consisted of Generals Hunter, Hitchcock, King, Prentiss, Ricketts, Casey, N. B. Buford, Slough and Garfield. Under their finding and sentence, approved by President Lincoln, he was cashiered and disqualified from holding office under the Government.

It was natural that General Porter should devote his life to obtaining a reversal of the sentence. As soon as the war was over he began corresponding with officers of the Confederate army, aiming especially at procuring opinions from them that Lee had succeeded in concentrating his army on the 29th of August, 1862, before Porter had been able to get into co-operation or connection with the rest of our army under Pope, who was attacking Jackson on the heights above Groveton, in the battle known as 'the Second Bull Run. During General Grant's two terms of Presidency the newly-discovered evidence was submitted to him, but he declined to allow any steps to be taken looking toward a re-opening of the case.

In 1878, President Hayes yielded to Porter's solicitations and appointed an Advisory Board, consisting of Generals Schofield, Terry and Getty, to examine the case, in view of the newly-discovered evidence claimed by Porter, and to report recommendations to the President. The anomalous character of such a Board, its legality, and its power to compel attendance of witnesses, are questions upon which I do not propose to touch. I shall confine myself wholly to matters in which you as a Society of military men of large experience in actual war will be interested. The Advisory Board found that Porter's conduct, so far from being blameworthy, was a model of military excellence, and advised that he be reinstated in the regular army with such rank as he would have reached in ordinary course if he had survived the war, with pay and emoluments for the score of years during which he had been remanded to civil life. The President referred the whole subject to Congress. A bill has been introduced this winter to carry out in substance the recommendation of the Advisory Board. The death of President Garfield gives opportunity for renewing the pressure for action upon his successor, and this is being vigorously used.

This outline of the situation, condensed as it is to the smallest compass, shows that the case is one on which the opinion of the men who themselves served in the war ought to be felt, and no one can question the right of associations like this to lead their fellow-citizens in the effort to reach a right judgment upon it.

My own convictions I will state as follows:

1. The so-called newly-discovered evidence gives us nothing worthy to overthrow or to modify the judgment of the Court-martial, which tried Porter in 1862. Rightly considered, it sustains and supports that judgment in a strong and striking manner.

2. Lapse of time has greatly increased the unreliability of mere memory, especially as to hours of the day; and as Porter's case rests largely upon this sort of memory, the Court-martial convened in the very year of his alleged misconduct was much more likely to have trustworthy evidence than the Advisory Board.

3. The new evidence is almost wholly from Confederate sources; and that part of it which is orig-

inal and was contemporaneous with the events, is overwhelmingly in support of the condition of facts found by the Court-martial.

4. The question of Porter's guilt turned upon his conduct under the orders he received, and in view of the situation at the time as he and his commander knew or had the means of knowing it. From this point of view, also, the Court-martial was right and the Advisory Board was wrong.

5. To accept the present statements from memory of the Confederate officers as to the time and place of Longstreet's arrival on that field, still leaves the most inextricable confusion and contradiction among them, with a decided balance in favor of those who agree with the conclusions drawn from the general concurrence of witnesses who were in the National army, and whose testimony supports the judgment of the Court-martial.

6. If Porter were right as to time and place of Longstreet on the field, the judgment of the Court-martial against him would still be sound on military principles.

To discuss the whole campaign of August, 1862, is plainly impossible within the limits of a single paper. To discuss the whole series of engagements in the last days of that month would carry me beyond the limits of a single evening. I shall have to confine myself to the events upon which the

Court-martial of 1862 based their judgment, namely, those occurring on the 28th and 29th of the month, and on these I must assume that you are familiar with the general history.

The Advisory Board found that Porter's *animus* towards General Pope, his commander, was of no real importance in the case. I confess myself unable to comprehend how this was possible. The spirit and intention constitutes the difference between a man's foolishly being captured by the enemy and his being a deserter deserving death. It constitutes the essential difference between an officer's doing some blundering or timid thing, deserving only censure or contempt, and his being guilty of the highest of military crimes. The stern law of war punishes even cowardice with death when it sets a dangerous example; but if a hostile spirit of hatred and insubordination toward the commander produces the same results as cowardice would, the crime is exaggerated. In the one case it may be a physical weakness, which we pity and despise, while we punish it; in the other it is a purposed and willful wrong, allied closely to treachery. To say that malice makes no difference in offenses, is simply to invert all rules. I must say, therefore, at the start, that if any one holds that Porter's *animus* toward his superior officer ought not to weigh in considering his conduct under his orders, from him I must part company at the very beginning; for I hold most explicitly that express ill-will and insubordination being once proven, it must necessarily affect our interpretation of conduct in every situation of the day.

MARCH FROM WARRENTON JUNCTION, AUGUST 27–'8.

The manner in which one judges of Porter's delay in obeying the order to march from Warrenton Junction to Bristow on the night of the 27–28th of August will, to some extent, determine his standpoint in judging of things which occurred later.

The order from Pope to Porter was an explicit one: "The Major-General commanding directs that you start at 1 *o'clock to-night* and come forward with your whole corps . . . *so as to be here by day-light* to-morrow morning." It said Hooker had been in a severe engagement. It indicated an advantage over the enemy, but not a rout. It repeated: "It is necessary on all accounts that you should be here by daylight." The general facts were that the most enterprising officer of the Confederate army, with nearly half of Lee's infantry and all his cavalry, was upon the line of our communications. It was a time when extraordinary speed of movement and rapidity of combination was plainly demanded on our side; a time when, if ever, a commanding officer needed to feel his troops answering like a spirited charger to the spur; a crisis in which a supreme exertion may rightly be demanded of every officer and man composing an army. It was a summer night, the roads were dry; and, so far as physical comfort went, the troops could march easier than by day; but no matter for that, the order indicated fighting for the next day, and was peremptory as to time of starting. Porter did not obey it, but began his march at daylight, the time when he was ordered to arrive at Bristow. His excuse was that the night was dark, that one of his divisions had had a hard march that day, and that from such reports as he had, the road to Bristow was a good deal obstructed by wagons. The sufficiency of the excuse can not be admitted. It might do for a peaceful march, away from the presence of the enemy; but in war and in such a crisis in war, our judgment must refuse to assent to the justification. Let us see how other soldiers judged of their duty in similar circumstances. In Georgia, on the 25th of May, 1864, the Twenty-third Corps was marching late in the evening, trying to reach Pumpkin-vine Creek, after crossing the Etowah River. Hooker was in advance, and his trains in this case also filled the road. The column was necessarily broken, the men picking their way among the wagons, straggling out by the road-side when it was possible to march there, and being wearied and worried to the last degree by the obstacles. Just before dark distant firing was heard. Schofield ordered that the column should close up and push on as fast as possible. A severe thunder-storm came up, followed by pouring, drenching rain, in which the corps continued to march till midnight, and then went into bivouac by the road-side, not a wagon or tent of their own being near them. Instead of seeking shelter, General Schofield himself pushed forward to see what had been going on; and in trying to pass some wagons his horse fell with him into a gully which could not be seen in the darkness, and he was severely hurt. But orders were sent for the corps to continue its march, after only a single hour of rest they marched again, and the gray in the east was just appearing when they reported to Sherman and asked for an assignment of their position on the field. Hooker had had, as in 1862, a very severe action, though it was at New Hope Church this time. There was no council of division officers called to consider the propriety of marching, but orders were issued and the march was made, and every soldier knows that it is only in that way that campaigns are made successful.

It is a telling sarcasm on Porter's conduct that he was, at Warrenton Junction that very day, writing to Burnside that no vigor was shown by Pope's command; that the enemy was "pursuing his route *unmolested* to the Shenandoah;" that he found "a vast difference between these troops (the Army of Virginia) and ours;" and that they "needed some good troops to give them heart, and, I think, head!"

Whatever good services Porter had done before, gave to his new commander the right to expect ability and efficiency from him; and when we see him, day after day, sneering at Pope, and, as in the letter quoted above, basing his sneers at Pope's ignorance of the situation upon an ignorance of his own, more glaring in contrast with the facts as history now reveals them to us, than anything to be found in Pope's dispatches, we find ourselves concluding that General T. C. H. Smith was, on the whole, right in interpreting Porter's animus as he did, and in saying that Pope might expect him to fail him. It is only just to judge what occurred on the 29th of August in the light of this conduct and of this spirit.

No doubt military orders are to be taken according to the spirit rather than the letter, and that a certain discretion belongs to a corps or division commander; but the danger is that this discretion will be made the pretext for doing less than he is ordered to do. It would be safer to say that discretion is left the subordinate to do more, but rarely to do less than ordered, if the thing is possible. A commanding officer will be forced to put his orders in curt and peremptory phrase always, if his subordinates are to find reasons in his explanation for doing as much or as little as they please. There may be good reasons why a dispatch shall conceeal the true reasons for an order. It is rarely wise to say any thing which could do harm if it fell into the enemy's hands, and any dispatch may do so. In the presence of an enemy a subordinate is never justifiable in drawing reasons from the narrative part of a dispatch for neglecting the mandatory part. He is bound to assume that his superior had good reasons for his order, and knew as well as he who receives it, that there may be apparent inconsistency between the thing commanded and the situation as partly described. Pope's reiterated and emphatic assertion of the necessity of Porter's presence by daylight meant, and could only mean, that the advantage Hooker was said to have was still consistent with *some* imminent danger, or some imperative necessity in regard to proposed action. We can not ignore or forget that every body knew the situation was a very grave one. Porter's own dispatches show that he knew the rest of Lee's army was forcing the marching to join Jackson, and that a series of engagements had already begun which must end in the disgrace, if not ruin of the National army, unless every corps and division commander exhibited the fullest energy of which he was capable. And the delay of Wednesday night does not stand alone. It was followed by the order to march at first blush of dawn on the 29th, receipted for at half-past five but not obeyed till seven. The interval was used on that morning, *not* in writing a dispatch to Pope saying that the order was received after the contemplated hour of movement, but he would try to make up for the delay by instantaneous marching and increase of speed,—no, instead of this Porter is writing at six a long letter to Burnside, repeating his sneers at Pope's assumed ignorance of the situation, talking of his taking two corps to Centerville as a "body guard," when the dispatch in his hand showed that Pope had not moved with these corps to Centerville at all, but was at Bull Run. He says to his correspondent: "Comment is unnecessary," when that phrase is to be used, if at all, by those who consider *his* conduct under such circumstances. He exhibits himself plainly as a disaffected subordinate, writing professional libels on his superior, while he neglected and delayed obedience in so systematic a way as to demonstrate that his commander was likely to fail in any combination which depended on his promptness or efficiency.

### DISCREPANCIES IN TESTIMONY.

In considering testimony of the kinds presented to us in this record we should keep in mind the fact that much of it is the remembrance of men after sixteen years has elapsed. No one will claim that this is as reliable as contemporaneous evidence. It would be a miracle if much were not lost, much misremembered after that lapse of time. In recalling events so remote, a natural law of memory will give length of duration relatively great to those occurrences in a given day which seem most important.

Again, judgment as to the hour of day, is, after a long interval, one of the most uncertain of things, unless there is something like the peculiar light of dawn, of twilight, of gathering darkness, etc., associated in the memory with the picture itself, and so helping to fix the time. Dispatches noting the hour of sending, or indorsed with the hour of receipt, are among the most reliable fixed points from which we can reckon, and should outweigh other evidence as to time, when such dispatches seem to be sent in the ordinary course of business, and are free from suspicion of being made for a purpose.

Men mean to perjure themselves much less frequently than people think, and palpable inaccuracies in testimony on immaterial points, are quite consistent with the general truth of a statement. We have swift witnesses who really think they remember every thing the counsel who calls them may insinuate, and we have others who are easily led into the trap of testifying to immaterial details on which they have no clear memory. The case before us illustrates both these phases of inaccuracy. The orderlies who accompanied Captain Douglass Pope in carrying the 4:30 order were readily led to say they remembered a steeple on Bethlehem Church, a thing easily accounted for by the firm association of a steeple with a church in the minds of most Northern men. Porter's counsel argued that here was proof of false swearing, but they do not seem to have noticed that, of the two witnesses called to contradict the orderlies, and who tell us they had known the church all their lives, one testifies that the church was a frame building, and the other that it was built of brick.*

So, also, Porter called a number of very respectable witnesses, including General Morell, to discredit the cavalry officer commanding the detachment which accompanied the troops in the move-

---

* The volumes and pages referred to in the foot-notes are those of the Congressional publication of the proceedings. (Vol. 3, p. 1116.

ment to Dawkins Branch, and who, in substance, deny that any such cavalry detachment was present. Yet, in the very opening statement of counsel was read a dispatch from Porter to Morell that day, asking to have some of "that cavalry" sent back to him at Bethlehem Church.*

Of the swift witness kind is the staff officer who insisted that he carried reports direct from Colonel Marshall on the skirmish line to Porter frequently during the afternoon of the 29th, and that Porter was nearly all the time at the immediate front, when nothing is better settled than that soon after McDowell left, Porter went back to Bethlehem Church on the forks of the Sudley road and stayed there till evening.†

We have to discriminate as to the value of testimony under all such circumstances, but it is not necessary to assume willful lying on the part of witnesses. After so long a time, memory and imagination get easily mixed, and this is no small objection to opening so old a case.

### THE QUESTION OF THE TIME OF LONGSTREET'S APPEARANCE ON THE 29TH.

In view of the difficulties which surround the case, it is very desirable to fix some conclusive and satisfactory starting point in determining the very

---

*Vol. 3, p. 33.   †Vol. 2, p. 416.

important questions of time on the 29th. It would seem that it may best be found in the arrival of Heintzelman's corps on the field and in the movement of Poe's brigade around Jackson's left flank. The very fact that this was the opposite extreme of the field from Porter, and that the hours are fixed without reference to him, makes the testimony disinterested as well as trustworthy.

Heintzelman came on the field about ten in the morning, and tells what was then going on, including the movement of Kearney's division in which was Poe's brigade. This is fixed by the entry made at the very hour in Heintzelman's diary, and is accepted by every body. Poe is thus shown to be right in his statement of the time of his effort to outflank Jackson's left. He deployed between the Matthews house and the Sudley road after ten o'clock and moved forward, crossing Bull Run, and so far succeeded in his purpose as to create confusion and dismay for a time in Jackson's rear. This can not have been earlier than half-past ten, considering the character of the movement, and Porter's counsel recognize this fact by dating Poe's position near Sudley Church on the map accompanying their argument, at eleven o'clock. Here, then, we have a fixed point about which there is no dispute. Let us hold fast to it.*

---

* Vol. 2, p. 580.

General J. E. B. Stuart, in the memorandum attached to his report, says he was there when this attack was made; that he gave the directions for some of his artillery and troops to resist it; names the officers of both arms, one of whom was mortally wounded; states the time as about ten, and tells us that after the flurry was over he started to find Longstreet.* Mark that this was contemporaneous evidence, both Heintzelman's diary and Stuart's report, and made without the remotest reference to Porter. It is corroborated by witnesses from both the Confederate and the National armies in the most abundant way, but it does not need corroboration. If we know any thing about that field, we know that Stuart started from the scene of Poe's attack to find Longstreet, not earlier than half-past ten o'clock, and probably as late as eleven. He took with him a considerable body of cavalry, Robertson's brigade at least, and rode by way of Catharpin Valley around Jackson's rear, thence across the country to Gainesville, and out toward Thoroughfare Gap, meeting the head of Longstreet's column between Gainesville and Haymarket. Adopting, therefore, the time fixed by Porter and his counsel as that of Poe's affair on our extreme right (eleven o'clock), taking also into ac-

---

* Vol. 2, p. 359.

count the ordinary rate at which a large body of horse would move in marching, as Stuart marched, and looking to the distance they had to go, it is quite within bounds to say it took Stuart an hour and a half to get to the point named; and that, therefore, the head of Longstreet's column was half-way between Haymarket and Gainesville at half-past twelve, certainly not earlier than noon. They were then two hours' ordinary march from Jackson's right at the Douglass house, and it would take forced marching to reach there in an hour and a half. It would seem proven, therefore, that they could not, and did not, make connection with Jackson before half-past one. The simple chain of evidence which leads to this conclusion seems decisive, and it best harmonizes a host of other facts. It is also most in accord with the best contemporaneous evidence of other sorts on both sides.

Remember that Lee had no cavalry but what was with Jackson, that Longstreet had Ricketts' division in front of him, opposing his advance during the evening before, and had no reason to suppose his road was clear in the morning; that he must have skirmished—nay, that he did skirmish carefully forward, as Hood's report shows; and that Cadmus Wilcox, who came by the other gap, says, in his official report, that he reached the junction of the roads *west* of Haymarket at half-past nine, and found Longstreet's column just passing there.* This in itself makes absurd the Buford dispatch on which so much has been built by Porter, and destroys it, except as evidence that Buford wrote it at half-past nine upon mistaken information.† Whilst Hood says that he himself got on the field earlier, he puts the time when the whole of Longstreet's column arrived at two o'clock. ‡ These and many other collateral things go to establish the fact as above stated, but it is time to hasten to the next step, which is to see how far the independent line of proof taken from the movements of Schenck and Reynolds forces us to the same conclusion.

### SCHENCK'S AND REYNOLDS' MOVEMENTS ON THE MORNING OF THE 29TH.

What has been said above sufficiently indicates that Longstreet went forward cautiously, and therefore slowly, till he met Stuart; then, getting the latest news, and learning of Jackson's necessity, he hastened the marching, while Stuart, with a detachment of the cavalry, galloped, as Blackford says, to the place near Hampton Cole's, on the Monroe Hill, where Rosser, with one regiment of

---

* Vol. 2, 535; vol. 1, p. 472.

† N. B. Buford, who was on the Court-martial, was half-brother of him who sent the dispatch. It can not be said that it was not likely to have all due weight given to it.

‡ Vol. 1, p. 552.

cavalry, was keeping Porter from advancing by his demonstrations, and by the dust which his troopers raised by dragging the brush in the road.*

Let us now look at the center of the field. It is clear that though Sigel's forces were moving earlier, the slow character of Schenck's advance, as he describes it, made it about noon when he swung forward from the woods bordering Lewis Lane, No. 1. Benjamin's testimony is conclusive on this point. He commanded a battery of regulars, and belonged to the Ninth Corps, which came on the ground about noon, as appears from Heintzelman's diary, and he was ordered to report to Schenck, to assist in his movement then in progress. He identifies the ridge just east of Groveton where his battery went into position, his right on the pike. He mentions the enemy's skirmishers in front of and to the west of him, which were driven out. He says he placed his battery about half-past twelve, that after a few shots all was quiet for an hour, then a severe artillery fire was opened from the direction of the Douglass house, and the cannonade lasted till late in the afternoon, when he had to withdraw his battery to repair damages and reorganize.† This covers the whole period of Schenck's movement, and his

---

\* Vol. 2, pp. 673, 678; vol. 3, p. 1073.
† Vol. 2, p. 608.

return to the road east of Lewis Lane, where he covered the position of the battery and remained, as he testifies, till four o'clock or later. Schenck is not only corroborated by General McLean, Major Fox and others, but a decisive fact is found in their going through the well identified wood where Gibbon's field hospital was after the fight of the night before, and where Schenck had those still living cared for and sent to the rear. No more intelligent or unimpeachable witnesses could be found than those who thus testify. Schenck, every body knows. McLean is a son of the late Judge McLean, of the United States Supreme Court; Major Fox is a well known business man of high standing in Cincinnati; and Colonel Benjamin, now Assistant Adjutant General at Washington, served both in the East and in the West, and was well known as one of the coolest and bravest officers of artillery in the army.

But Reynolds' division was on Schenck's left and went forward also. General Meade commanded one of his brigades. Reynolds was Porter's friend, had served in his command before Richmond, and both he and Meade were men who could not be charged with making careless or false reports of their part in the engagement. Reynolds reports that he crossed the pike, pushing forward to turn Jackson's right, and continued the movement till Longstreet came on the field, and artillery opened upon him in rear of his left flank.* Meade told McLean in person that he had got into a hornet's nest of batteries. Other testimony shows that they retired only because they were too late to accomplish their purpose.

If we let Schenck occupy the Gibbon woods and extend Meade on that flank, with the rest of Reynolds' division beyond him, even if somewhat refused, it is plain that they must have occupied the high ground at and beyond the Cundliffe house. Reynolds himself says he had partial possession of the highest ground south of the pike when the Confederate battery was put in, viz., the Monroe or Stuart Hill, near the pike.† He subsequently saw what Schenck's report said of his retiring, and in his correspondence with Colonel Cheesbrough, of Schenck's staff, as well as in his own testimony, he distinctly says that Longstreet's troops were not deployed across the pike till one o'clock or sometime in the afternoon. He corrects Cheesbrough by asserting that it was not till *late* in the afternoon, towards dusk, that Longstreet's deployment was so complete as to outflank him on the left, after this wing had been drawn back.‡ He says his artillery, supported by Meade, engaged Jackson on the same

---

* Vol. 2, p. 506.
† Vol. 1, p. 167.
‡ Vol. 1, pp. 166, 167; Vol. 2. p. 507.

ridge they were on, till his position was made untenable by the approach of Longstreet on the pike.

As to the time of Longstreet's arrival, therefore, this independent mode of determining it corroborates the former. The testimony of Benjamin establishes the fact that the re-enforcements in artillery, which went into position on Jackson's right, and which, as we know from Longstreet, were his batteries, came into action between one and two o'clock, and were added to for some time later. Reynolds plainly insists that he did not begin to withdraw till after these re-enforcements arrived; his subordinates, together with Schenck, McLean and their subordinates, confirm this view.

It is the connection of these things with definite and fixed starting points that gives them their force, and when we find that Reynolds and Schenck, without knowledge of where Stuart was or what he was doing, give us the same conclusion as to the time of Longstreet's arrival, that we deduce from Poe's affair on the right and Stuart's subsequent ride toward Haymarket, and when an independent estimate reached from a still different starting point in Benjamin's case, brings us to the same result, no amount of subsequent guessing at the time can change it. Now add the time it would take to deploy and put in position the whole of Longstreet's command after the head of the column came up, and it could not have been earlier than three, it was quite likely to be as late as four, when his right reached the Manassas and Gainesville road on which Porter was.

It will be seen, by and by, that Porter gave no new cause for anxiety to Lee later in the afternoon, and Longstreet, being informed as he came up, of his being on their flank, sent Wilcox's division across, as soon as his connection with Jackson was safely made and he was assured that Reynolds had really given up his aggressive movement. But both Lee and Longstreet put this late in the day, and Wilcox's report and testimony say it was *half-past four.*\* This may fairly be said to fix the time when he had finished his deployment, and was at liberty to attend to other matters. It is not credible that he should not have sent Wilcox earlier if he had been in position before noon.

The fact that Rosser's cavalry dragged limbs of trees in the road to create the impression upon Porter that a large force was in front of him, neither has been nor can be contradicted. It has only been waved aside as of little consequence. It can not be properly treated so. Rosser says that he did it for several hours, and that it was done to deceive Porter. Stuart says in his official report that Porter's

---

\* Vol. 2, p. 535.

own report proved the success of the ruse. Chaplain Landstreet watched it with interest because he knew its purpose. The fact being undisputed, it is impossible to get away from its logical consequences. The ruse was practiced because Longstreet was not yet in position, and it was presumably continued until, and only until, the need of it was over, and the Confederate line was formed. It is one of those speaking facts which outweigh a world of those estimates of time from mere memory, for which General Gibbon sensibly testified that "he would not give a snap of his finger." It is not necessary to treat Rosser's estimate of three or four hours differently from other estimates. Take it simply that he continued it for so long a time that the best impression he now has is as he gives it, and it still seems a capital, if not a decisive fact in the case. If the time were only half what he thinks, it still shows that for some two hours after Rosser became aware of the presence of Porter's column, there was nothing but a little cavalry to prevent the latter from pushing over the hill at Hampton Cole's and Monroe's, and into close support of the movement Reynolds and Schenck were making.

Closely connected with this, and almost conclusive in itself, is the testimony of Major White of Stuart's staff. When Stuart reached the hill in front of Porter and saw what was going on, he sent

White to Jackson to report the Union troops coming on that road. If Longstreet had been between Stuart and Jackson, would White have been sent clear across Longstreet's front to the latter? Longstreet, therefore, had not yet arrived when Porter came to Dawkins branch, no matter what you call the hour, and Jackson on the hills north of the pike was the nearest Confederate commander to whom to send. But White, on his return from Jackson, took a short cut through the wood where Gibbon's dead and wounded lay. This shows that Schenck's advance had not yet reached there, or would make it so late as to show that Longstreet was some hours later in arriving than even General Pope has claimed. The circumstances show that it was before Schenck's movement, for White saw the artillery firing from Cole's toward Reynolds on that officer's advance over the same ground the witness had traveled in coming back from Jackson. But I do not intend to repeat here what has been presented in another form as a summary of evidence at this end of the line, but only to point out how solidly it supports that which is drawn in turn from our right, our center, and from the best reliable and fixed data given by Confederate witnesses.

### ERRORS IN RECOLLECTION.

At as early a day as 1866, General Porter began to collect from Confederate officers such letters as would favor his application for a reversal of his sentence. In October, 1867, he got from General R. E. Lee, a letter based on memory, which is one of the most convincing proofs of the unreliability of such recollection.* In it Lee puts the time of the arrival of Longstreet's head of column on the field as early as Cadmus Wilcox's official report proves it to have been at the Junction of the roads between Thoroughfare Gap and Haymarket, and an hour and a half earlier than Poe's attack on Jackson's left, which occurred before Stuart started on his seven-mile ride to meet Lee himself, with Longstreet, between Gainesville and Haymarket! Lee's estimate of about two and a half hours as the time it took Longstreet to get into position after the head of the column came up, is valuable as based on an expert's knowledge of the time such maneuvers would ordinarily take, and is totally different from the attempt to recollect a particular hour of the day. With such letters as this of Lee's, and some similar ones, it would be strange indeed if Porter and his counsel could not make other officers and men on

---

* Vol. 1. p. 551.

both sides modify their opinions. An example of this is found in Longstreet's admitted modification of former statements after talking with Porter's friends in attendance upon this investigation. Men naturally hesitate to put their recollection against that of others whom they respect, when the statements of these are pressed upon them. But fortunately for history there are facts and conjunctions of facts making logical chains to which *mere* memory is as a rope of sand. We may assume that the time of the occurrences that morning of the 29th has been shoved forward at least a couple of hours in the minds of nearly all the Confederate officers by the knowledge that those letters had been written, except where their own official reports or memoranda made at the time have saved them from doubting their own judgment. White, of Stuart's staff, seems to be one of the clearest and most consistent witnesses of the whole class, yet he, who was with Stuart at the time, under the influence of this epidemic of refreshed recollection as to hours, puts the affair with Poe near Sudley at eight or nine in the morning, though Stuart's report at the time said about ten, and Porter and his counsel now admit it was eleven, as has been shown. This error in starting must run, of course, through the middle of the day, at least, and until some new departure occurs to set it right. Such considerations as these give great strength to General Gibbon's estimate of the small value of memory as to the mere time of day in the midst of such exciting scenes, unless the recollection is helped by the fixed data to which reference has been made. It is therefore not merely because the concurrent evidence from several independent sources proves the arrival of Longstreet to have been much later than the time when Porter reached Dawkins branch, but also because that fact, is not so dependent upon what is thus indicated as the most untrustworthy kind of evidence, that it should be regarded as overweighing the honest but most fallacious efforts to fix the time by recollection alone after so many years.

### LONGSTREET'S POSITION ON THE FIELD.

If Longstreet was not in position in front of Porter for four or five hours, or one or two hours even, after the latter reached Dawkins branch, his defense of his conduct fails. But the student of the field will desire to determine for himself what Longstreet's position on it was. There are difficulties in the way of a satisfactory conclusion, but the weight of evidence is largely in favor of putting him west of Page-land Lane.

Let us go back and study the topography of the field a little, which we may do, as to the greater part of it, by the aid of General Warren's map with contour lines of elevations, which is number six of the quarto volume accompanying the Board's report.

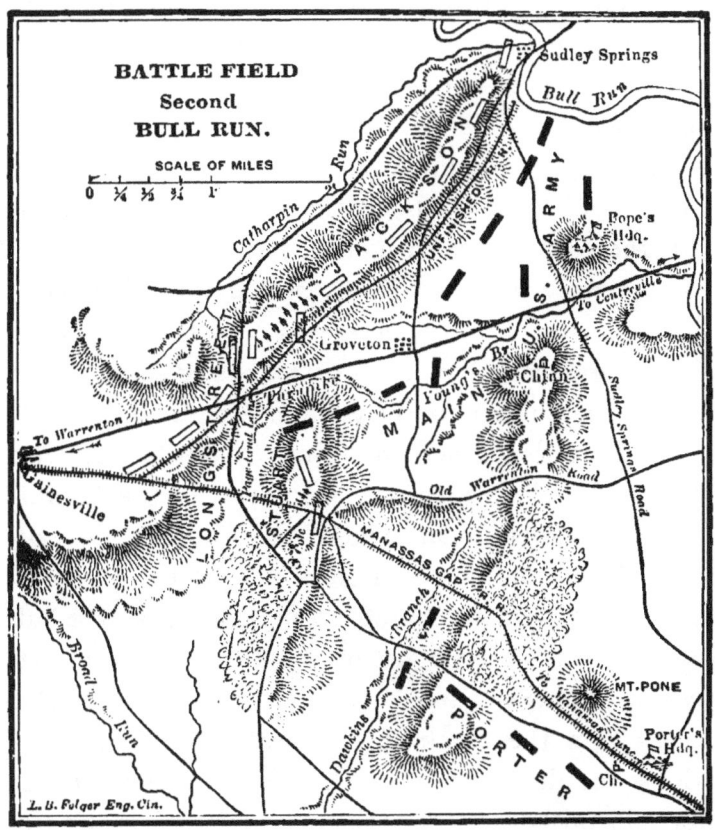

Porter's command was in the only considerable forest that was in the whole field of operations that day. Had he been out of it anywhere, he could hardly have failed to see what was going on. The country was undulating, the ridges being fifty or sixty feet only above the hollows in which the insignificant water-courses ran. The topographical lines nowhere show any deep ravines, nor any conformation which would prevent movements of an army in line of battle except in the wood already spoken of; and as to that, General Warren testified to what every military man could tell *a priori*, that there would be no difficulty in taking troops through it if the outskirts were held. It constituted, therefore, simply an obstruction in the way of maneuver, but had the advantage also of being a cover for the movement of Porter's troops as soon as the terrain was understood by the officer in command.

In Porter's immediate front, from the ridge on which Morell's troops were deployed to the Hampton Cole house, near which the Confederate cavalry officer put in a section of a light battery, is a distance of something more than a mile and a-half by the scale, with a hollow of only sixty feet between. The ground was open in the direct line west from the creek, but wooded to the left and along the dirt road, so as to afford excellent cover for skirmishers advancing. At the Cole house, which both the contour lines and the testimony show to be one of the most important points on the field, there is a convergence of roads. That by which Porter was advancing, the Manassas Gap

Railway, the old Warrenton and Washington road by which McDowell's left would naturally have gone into position, a lane from the Gainesville pike, and a road from Bristow Station (General Banks' position), all meet at that point.

From the Monroe house, on the crest a little further west, the view reached as far as Gainesville, and revealed every thing between there and Pope's head-quarters at Buck Hill. Here was Stuart's position beyond all doubt, and the elevation bears his name in the vicinity to this day. Chaplain Landstreet was there with him, and though the lack of fuller development of this part of the map made him refer Stuart's position to the Cole house, his testimony is clear and telling as to what he saw. The character of this position must be kept carefully in mind.

Morell's ridge slopes upward toward the east, to the crowning point called Mount Pone, a bald knob in the open, which is the only considerable elevation within the Union lines. On the slope behind Morell the contour line marked two hundred and ten runs, by a very direct course north, coming into the open ground where it crosses the old Warrenton and Washington road, before mentioned, and thence continues in an almost equally direct line to the Chinn house, where the slope descends to the Gainesville pike, near Pope's head-quarters. By a direct line, therefore, and on an exact level, going neither up hill nor down even so much as five feet, the position of Porter's advance division was connected with the position occupied by Sigel's corps that morning, the screen of woods alone preventing this from being plain to their eyes at the time.

But, again, the old Warrenton and Washington Road, leaving the Hampton Cole house, goes eastward along a ridge on almost exactly the same contour last mentioned, being a practically level road till it meets the prolongation of Morell's line of deployment extended northward. Near this point the road marked Compton's Lane goes off to Groveton, descending the slope and passing through the position in which Reynolds' division was that morning on the left of Schenck. Around the foot of the gentle slopes to the north runs Young's Branch, in the hollow which separated the position of the United States troops from those of Jackson, who lay on the still more commanding ground to the north, on a ridge forty or fifty feet higher than that which connected Schenck's with Porter's position.

The official maps made by General Warren, excellent as they are in other respects, are deficient in not extending the contours which mark the topography, so as to include the Monroe or Stuart

Hill, which is the crest of the high ground, of which Hampton Cole's is a part. The Judge Advocate presented one in argument, which indicated the topography further west toward Gainesville, but it was not before the witnesses when they testified, and was so ridiculed by Porter's counsel that one might well hesitate to trust to it, if General Porter himself, in a paper printed since the investigation, had not treated its topography as correct.

It is to be regretted that the witnesses were not referred to a map which showed the character of the ground at one of the most important points of the field. A witness who has before him what is treated as an official chart of the theater of operations is almost certainly led to place every thing within those limits, and this influence is manifest in the testimony of several. In the official map this absence of contour lines west of Hampton Cole's gives to that point the appearance of being the crest from which Gainesville was visible. Witnesses would naturally be led to speak of that as the crest, which, in fact, was a little farther west, at Monroe's. This, however, makes no material difference in the conclusion to be drawn from the testimony, as may easily be made apparent.

Let us extend our examination of the field over the portion not contoured by General Warren. The natural starting point is at the Douglass house near the right of Jackson's line, and which is a prominent feature in all descriptions of the engagement. That house stands on the slope running from the contour line marked 220 feet to that marked 240 feet. Going south-westerly along the general line of the ridge which formed Jackson's position, we find ourselves on a continuing hill, of which the crest is about five hundred yards wide between the contours marked 220 on the two sides of it.

This ridge, thus directly continuing Jackson's position, crosses the pike and keeps the same direction south-west for three-quarters of a mile, till it reaches the Manassas Gap Railroad, which is there on the top of the watershed dividing the streams flowing southward into Broad Run and towards Bristow, from those flowing northward into Catharpin Run (behind Jackson), and into Young's Branch. Immediately in rear of the place last named, and toward Gainesville, the ground rises again above the contour marked 240, and even 260, and forms an almost semicircular ridge with its two flanks on the pike, and its face southward in the direction of Bristow. If the larger ridge last described were occupied by a line of battle, no military man will fail to see at once the strength of this position for a refused flank on his extreme right, if there were the slightest reason to apprehend the approach of an enemy from any point between south and west—from Bristow to the direction of Warrenton. The position thus described is crossed by no ravine or water-course. It has in front the hollow in which runs the upper part of Young's Branch, which makes an elbow, and crosses the pike twice, bearing away to the south-east, toward the Lewis-Leachman house. On the north side of the pike the continuation of the same contour level comes forward like a bastion or salient in the line till it reaches the edge of the "Gibbon Woods," to which reference has so often been made. Nearly the whole front of this position, from the pike southward, is covered by a screen of woods, the open crest behind being thus admirably placed for easiest and most concealed maneuver, whilst the open front which stretches southward from a point a little west of the Douglass house gives the needed sweep for the artillery which was placed there. The smaller map used by Porter's counsel in argument and numbered 16, shows two things more clearly than the larger ones, viz: the relation of the branch of Catharpin Run to the parallel part of Young's Branch, and the continuation of the unfinished line of railway till it unites with the Manassas Gap Railroad. The latter very significantly indicates to any one having an eye for topography, that the natural continuation of Jackson's position was along the same line of railroad survey upon the ridge which has just been described.

Such considerations make it almost certain that when Lee came on a field where Jackson was already warmly pressed by a force which the commanding General believed to be equal or superior to his own, he would form his right wing on this plain prolongation of Jackson's formation, unless something in the character and position of the Monroe Hill should forbid. It is not necessary to assume that Lee would mean to stay permanently where he formed his line of battle. His tactics were quite as likely to be aggressive in those days as ours. We must remember, too, that Stuart already held the highest part of this saddle-shaped Monroe Hill, and that it is called by his name in the neighborhood now, from the fact that he took his station on the southern end of it with his horsemen, after he came back from his meeting with Lee and Longstreet, on the Haymarket road. The middle part of the ridge is no higher than the corresponding part of the one west of Page-land Lane, which has been described above. The northern part, which runs up to the contour line 240, is narrow; its length is north and south, and *both sides of it are completely enfiladed* by the batteries, which, it is admitted, were massed in the interval between Jackson and Longstreet and near the Douglass house. These were Meade's "hornets' nest." That salient would have proved as useful to the Confederate artillery if an attack by the left center of our forces had been made on Longstreet's right after he was fairly in position, as it proved the next day when the artillery was massed upon Porter in his attack at our right center. Lee could, therefore, perfectly well afford to neglect occupying the Monroe Hill till he was fully assured that there was no danger impending on his extreme right and rear. It is toward that direction we must turn our thoughts for a moment to appreciate his conduct.

Lee had left Pope in his old front on the Rappahannock when he started to follow Jackson in the bold movement on the rear of the National army. He knew, also, that the Army of the Potomac was on its way to join Pope. As Jackson had the cavalry with him, Lee had to act on faith and not on sight till he reopened communications with his subordinate at or after the passing of Thoroughfare Gap. All that either he or Jackson knew or could know was that the United States army was concentrating; but he was necessarily ignorant of the extent to which this had been effected. Is it not certain, therefore, that the line of railroad from Warrenton to Manassas must have represented to him the general line of the army under Pope, whilst the doubtful point to be settled was whether it had concentrated? Lee's anxiety on this subject is shown by the promptness with which he pushed some cavalry toward Warrenton to find out whether Pope still had forces there, and his doubts were not solved till the night of the 29th, when he got his report.* During the day of that date he was therefore necessarily influenced in his movements and in choosing his position, by the contingency of attack from the west as well as south. This view of the case so palpably occupied his mind and his subordinates' that by a sort of common consent they speak of Porter's column as coming from the direction of Bristow, which was the direction of shortest approach from the general line of Pope's army, as has been shown. They even allowed this natural theory of the situation to outweigh the fact that those of Porter's troops which they saw were on the Manassas road. Basing our judgment, therefore, on the most solid and fundamental facts in the general problem, we must conclude that it would be the natural and the wise thing for Lee to do in his situation, to extend Jackson's line on the continuous ridge, keeping the still higher ground commanding the Gainesville

---

* Vol. 2, p. 545. Report of Maj. Hairston.

pike and the Bristow road as the strong point to be occupied in force, if a serious push at him were made either from Warrenton or from Bristow. It is clear, also, that this high ground was that which Early had occupied in the morning, before the arrival of Longstreet, to cover Jackson's flank from apprehended dangers of precisely the same sort.

With this view of the situation, with the certainty that Ricketts had withdrawn toward Bristow, with the presumption that King's division had done the same, with the probability that Banks and the rest of Pope's army would be in the same direction (as was the fact), with the knowledge that one of the corps of the Army of the Potomac had come on the field from Centerville (Heintzelman's) as Jackson must have learned from his prisoners, Lee must almost necessarily have concluded that he was to have Pope's Army of Virginia on his front and right, and the Army of the Potomac on his left. On true military theory, therefore, Lee's line would be where it is placed above. If he had made a crochet at Jackson's right and put Longstreet on the line reaching thence to Hampton Cole's, his right wing would have been "in the air," sticking out like a sore thumb in a position to be most easily hurt. When he had settled the fact that his right and right front were not threatened, or that his forces were greatly superior in number or in *morale* to

Pope's, he could afford to advance that wing for decisive attack, as he did next day, but he would be quite unlikely to do it at once upon his arrival on the field. We must consider the testimony in the light of these probabilities when we strive to reconcile conflicts in the memory or the opinions of the witnesses in the case.

Hood tells us in his report that he formed on the extension of Jackson's line,* leaving a gap for the massing of the artillery. Wilcox fixes his own place in support of the artillery and behind the ridge. Both these positions are properly described only by taking the line we have selected. Stuart, as we have already seen, occupied the south end of the Monroe Hill. Neither he nor any one who was with him, says that Longstreet's formation was in front of that ridge. On the contrary, White and Blackford, his staff officers, Chaplain Landstreet of his command, and Colonel Rosser, all locate Longstreet's line behind Pageland Lane. Citizen Monroe, who lived on the hill, and was there that day, describes the "skirmishers" who were around his house (meaning probably Stuart's men), and says they were in front toward Hampton Cole's, but he places the line of battle of Longstreet behind Pageland Lane also, and says that none of these troops

---

* Vol. 2, p. 534.

went forward to the east of his house till the middle of the afternoon, when Hunton's brigade did so. * Hunton was a resident of that vicinity, and is the recent member of Congress from that district. The naming of his brigade by Monroe is therefore doubly important, because it was one in which were his neighbors, and which he would be likely to know well. Now we know from Lee's and Longstreet's reports that Hunton was ordered forward to support Hood in the contest between him and McDowell's men on the pike that evening, and this makes Monroe's testimony strongly corroborative of the rest. Citizen Carraco, whose house was nearest of all to Porter's front and a little east of Hampton Cole's, was at home all day till about four P. M., when, on warning from the Confederate officers, he went to the rear going past Cole's and up the railroad toward Gainesville about a mile.† He crossed no line of the enemy and saw none but a few cavalrymen with a single cannon a little in the rear of Cole's. If the Confederate line had been where Longstreet and some others, guessing at it, drew it on the map, he must necessarily have crossed it, as he must also have done if it had been anywhere on a possible position in front of that which has been indicated. All the

---

\* Vol. 2. p. 925. † Vol. 2. p. 921.

evidence given us by the reports of Reynolds and Schenck and the testimony of their subordinates is very strong in the same direction; indeed, it is irreconcilable with any other conclusion. The testimony of Colonel Marshall, who commanded Porter's skirmish line, is decisive to the same effect, if his testimony is worth any thing. He was brought forward as a peculiarly trustworthy and important witness by General Porter and his counsel on several occasions. His testimony was taken in the original trial, when he was on what was supposed was his death-bed from wounds received in battle. This fact was somewhat dramatically brought out to add to the solemn weight of his testimony. Stress was laid upon the fact that he was a regular officer, educated at West Point, and his opinions were put forward as if those of an expert. Most of this has an unpleasant air of clap-trap, but it certainly shows that his testimony must be taken as final by those who called him, when he speaks of military positions which he says he saw with his own eyes. His opinion that it was unsafe for Porter to attack under the half-past four o'clock order was said to be itself enough to exonerate his commander. If his testimony is good as to his fears, it certainly should be good as to his facts. He says that at *three o'clock in the afternoon,* or later, the enemy developed an infantry force, *the first infantry he had seen in his front,* about a mile north-west of the point near the Randall's house, (a little south of Hampton Cole's) where he himself crawled to make his observation.* A simple measurement of a mile north-west from the point where he placed himself, puts Longstreet's command again beyond Page-land Lane. If this force appeared there at three o'clock or later, and was the first infantry seen in Porter's front (and nobody else even pretends to have seen any), it demonstrates that Porter might have occupied that hill from Cole's to Monroe's for three or four hours at least, and have perfected his connection with the rest of the line long before Longstreet came dangerously near to him. As Marshall, therefore, from his command on the skirmish line, was the man upon whom Porter depended for the facts regarding the situation, and whom, as he claims, he trusted implicitly, he must be held to have known that Longstreet's line of battle was nowhere near the Hampton Cole house.

It agrees also with Longstreet's official report, in which he says that "late in the day" he heard of the Union troops on his left flank and sent three brigades there. All the Confederate witnesses agree that no man of their infantry on Porter's front was engaged that day. With one accord they say it

---

* Vol. 2, p. 132.

was only the cavalry vedettes that had a skirmish, and that so slight a one that we hear of no casualties on either side on the skirmish line.

Following Longstreet's line back again toward Jackson, we find the Confederate General Wilcox testifying that his division was placed 400 yards in rear of the artillery which was on the crest between Longstreet and Jackson; and when, after the combat with McDowell's troops that evening, he was withdrawn, he not only says it was to a position forming connection between Lee's two wings, but that this intervening space was a ridge behind which they could be sheltered.* We can find on the map nothing which answers to this description except the connecting ridge which has been described, and on which Longstreet's line has been located. Law, of Hood's division, who seems to have borne, on the Confederate side, the brunt of the fight on the pike that evening, says that in the night he withdrew to the position he occupied in the morning.† This corroborates the conclusion drawn from Wilcox's testimony.

In opposition to all this is the opinion of several Confederate officers which does not seem to be based upon any such decisive identification of localities.

---

\* Vol. 2, p. 266.     † Vol. 2, p. 542.

Their opinion can not be accepted without rejecting that of Reynolds and Schenck and their subordinates, upon points where it is quite incredible that they should be mistaken. We should have to reject, also, the testimony of a greater number of Confederate officers, who had better opportunities of knowing the exact facts in relation to the position of their right, besides the citizens whose testimony has been referred to.

But the assumption of the line at Hampton Cole's has difficulties of quite another sort. Jones, whose division is supposed to be on the brow of the hill immediately facing Porter, makes no reference to Porter's existence in his official report. Neither does Kemper. The testimony, which comes from witnesses who were in their commands, all indicates that they were not in Porter's presence at all. Drayton's brigade was put out at right angles to Jones' line, in support of Robertson's cavalry, late in the day; and this circumstance, which is clearly intelligible if Jones was where we have placed him, would be utterly unintelligible on the other hypothesis. With Jones at Hampton Cole's, his skirmishers should have been in contact with Porter, and he would have reported it. He not only does not report it, but officers from his command testify to the contrary. Yet Porter is supposed to have paralyzed the action of all these troops, which did not know of his existence.

Longstreet admits frankly that he don't know where to place Stuart and his cavalry, upon his theory of the field. But Stuart *is* placed beyond dispute where he would be behind and surrounded by the infantry if Longstreet is right, namely, on the Monroe or Stuart Hill. That is not where he was apt to be, and there is no scintilla of evidence that he sought such shelter. But Longstreet's effort to construct a theory favorable to Porter, involves him in other grave inconsistencies. In his letter, which Porter drew from him in 1866, he refused to state hours, and we have seen that he modified his opinions at this latest investigation after conference with Porter's friends. He now says he arrived with his head of column on the field about ten, having been in supporting distance since nine.* That is to say, a command stretched out three or four miles, as he says his was, is in supporting distance when the head of the column is some three miles away! Such support as that gave Napoleon many an opportunity to whip an enemy in detail. He says he was deployed within an hour (though Lee says it would take more than twice that time), and within twenty minutes thereafter, or

---

* Vol. 2, p. 117.

by twenty minutes past eleven, he made a personal reconnoissance to the Lewis-Leachman (more probably Cundliffe) house. That on his return, and while telling Lee what he saw, Stuart's report of Porter's advance reached him.* This would be, say half-past eleven o'clock. But when he is asked, in a subsequent part of the examination, the hour at which he got Stuart's report, he says two o'clock in the afternoon.† His official report, which says "late in the day," and Wilcox's report, which says half-past four, only enlarge the discrepancy and show the confusion of memory into which the conferences with Porter's friends had led him.

Again he says‡ that Porter delayed them, and that if they had had three or four more hours of light, they would have attacked. Waiving the fact that they actually made an attack at dusk, another indisputable fact is that they did not attack all the next day till the middle of the afternoon, though Porter was clean gone during the night. Still again he says§ that he did not know of Porter's withdrawal till next morning, when his official report, made at the time (and Stuart uses almost the same words), says that after a few shots Porter withdrew, moving around to Pope's front, and apparently join-

---

\* Vol. 2, pp. 120 and 129.  † Page 124.
‡ Page 121.   § Page 121.

ing in the attack on Jackson,* and when he shows also by both his report and his testimony that so far from Porter's holding his troops fast, he withdrew again Wilcox's division from his right, and used him in supporting Hood's attack in the center, which, being thus made with Hood's and Wilcox's divisions, and part of Kemper's, should be regarded as a general attack by him, for most of his command was thus put in, and the rest were ready to follow it up if he was successful. He admits failure of success, because he says he withdrew Hood on account of finding Pope's troops so heavily massed in his front.† To such a tissue of inconsistencies and contradictions does his benevolent disposition to help Porter bring him, and such is the valuable newly-discovered evidence on which the judgment of the Court-martial of 1862 is to be reversed. From whatever direction we approach the subject, therefore, we are brought to the same conclusion as to the time and place of Longstreet's deployment. The time was at least three or four hours after Porter reached Dawkins Branch, and the place was west of Page-land Lane.

### PORTER'S CONDUCT ON THE 29TH.

A written dispatch of General Sykes to General Morell, dated half-past eight on the morning of the

---
\* Vol. 2, p. 526.   † Ibid., p. 521.

29th, at Manassas Junction, says that the column was delayed while more ammunition was distributed. On the principle already stated, this date will be taken as a fixed point in that morning's history, and as showing that Porter's command was then at the Junction.

As to the delay itself, it appears in the testimony that the men then had forty rounds of ammunition with them,* and if speed was really meant, the need of waiting there to distribute more is at least questionable. In the west, the common way would have been to put the ammunition wagons into the column, and take other opportunities to distribute it, as the men's cartridge boxes were already full. We have no right to forget that, from the 26th onward, Pope's dispatches constantly urged haste. The one under which Porter was now acting repeated it. Every hour was of incalculable value as the event showed. But passing this by, we will assume that by nine o'clock Morell was leading off on the Gainesville road. The distances by scale seem to be a mile and a half to the forks of the Sudley road, where Porter's head-quarters were during the afternoon, and from there two miles to the ridge east of Dawkins Branch, where Morell deployed. From all the testimony as to the actual rate of marching, he

---

* Vol. 2, pp. 333 and 431.

ought to have been there in less than an hour and a half, and that would not be rapid work.  Some of the witnesses put the time of arrival at the branch as early as ten, but Porter claims that it was about eleven, and we may take it so, simply noting the fact that this certainly shows no excess of zeal in getting forward.  They had taken a prisoner or two, and had seen a citizen, and learned that some of the enemy's cavalry, a small number, were between them and Gainesville.  Skirmishers are thrown out and exchange a few harmless shots with Rosser's videttes. What ought Porter then to do?

To get rid of some fog, we must look at McDowell's relation to the command.  The famous "joint order" had directed him to follow Porter, and whilst they acted together, McDowell would, by virtue of seniority, have the right to command both corps, but this would be true only while they acted together and were beyond the immediate orders of the General-in-chief.  McDowell did not issue any orders to Porter up to the time he was with him in person at Dawkins Branch.  He was looking after King's division, which was in rather bad plight after its combat of the evening before, and the night retreat.  The "joint order," and Pope's special order to Porter were so far in accord that the latter was simply carrying out these directions, and was certainly bound to do so, in their full purpose and spirit, unless McDowell exercised his right to command by stopping him or modifying the order. Thus far no such thing had been done, and in speed of going forward, vigor of attacking any thing he should meet, and striving to do all that the order called for, he was as fully responsible till interfered with as if McDowell had not been there at all. He should, no doubt, have advised McDowell if he found any great force before him, but it can not be questionable that his business was to get into position alongside of his comrades, whose cannonade he heard in the direction of Groveton, and whose shells he and his troops saw bursting in the air when they came in front of the bit of open ground at Dawkins Branch. The indisputable fact that he never brushed away the cavalry skirmishers in his front, never developed any infantry of the enemy, and has to-day to rely upon conjecture and purely circumstantial evidence to prove that there was any infantry force immediately before him till late in the day, prove that he showed no vigor or energy whatever.

It seems to have been a full hour before McDowell came to Dawkins Branch in person, and there is no evidence of any dispatch or message from Porter to him. He seems to have found that Porter's column was halted, and then to have ridden forward to discover the cause. As it turned out, it is greatly to be regretted that McDowell did not remain and assume practical and efficient control of the movement on that line, but it is easy to understand how, in view of the difficulty of bringing up and deploying the whole force in the woods, he should have concluded that the "quickest way to apply his force to the enemy," was to go forward by the Sudley road whose forks were close to the head of his own column, and bring his men into line on Reynolds' left, where from his theory of the situation according to his map, he would probably be within easy communicating distance of Porter. He may have erred in judgment, but he did not retire to his tent. He acted, "he marched to the sound of the cannon," as the Comte de Paris says, and went as directly as possible toward his object, till he communicated with, and got new orders from his commanding General.

Had Porter "kept things moving," supporting his skirmishers properly, he would have been beyond the Hampton Cole house before McDowell came to the front, and the latter, in view of what he must have seen in five minutes' gallop on the Warrenton and Alexandria road around and east of Carraco's, could never have dreamed of any circuitous march to reach the field. It is the fatality of war that one blunder or fault involves many more. Porter was mentally and morally prepared to find the enemy before him, and from the moment his skirmishers exchanged shots with Rosser, he stopped stock-still, and never dreamed of another step in advance. By the time McDowell came up Rosser had set his wits to work, and the dust was rising from the brush his horsemen were dragging along the roads. Hearing Porter's report and seeing the dust, McDowell reached the conclusion that he could bring his men into action most speedily by way of the Sudley road, and hurried off for that purpose.

The testimony is not conclusive as to what were McDowell's parting orders to Porter, but the burden of proof is upon the latter to prove that they were explicit, that they contained directions he was bound to obey, and that they controlled his judgment in fact. McDowell testifies that he expected Porter to put his men into action there, but no soldier needs to be told that not even an explicit order from McDowell could continue to control Porter after the union of their forces, on which alone Porter's subordination was based, had been broken. Left to himself, his first duty as a soldier was to find out what was in front of him, and to do with energy what there was to do. A vigorous reconnoissance in force by a single brigade would have told the whole story in less than half an hour. Instead of this, even his skirmish line did not press the enemy, two or three cannon shots were exchanged, Porter went two miles to the rear, to his tent, and the quiet was only disturbed by the cannonade off to their right, where Jackson was wishing more earnestly for night or Longstreet than Wellington did for "night or Blucher."

Longstreet tells us that within twenty minutes from the time his line was formed he was down at the very verge of his skirmish line, making his own reconnoissance of the force in his front; but neither Porter, nor any division or brigade commander of his is found showing any curiosity in that direction. Is this what is to be expected of an energetic and faithful commander? We should grievously wrong the members of the Board if we should assume that they practiced upon the example which they officially declare is a model of all that is soldierly. It is a pleasure to note the different rules of duty they applied to themselves when important things were dependent on their action. When Schofield's little army was retreating from Columbia, Tennessee, the night before the bloody battle of Franklin, at the close of November, 1864, one of his subordinates, coming to Spring Hill with his command at midnight, sought the General to get further orders. Stanley told him that Schofield had taken the advanced guard and gone off to Thompson's Station to settle for himself the truth of the report that Forrest was already intercepting us at the forks of the road. This was not in the middle of a summer day, but in the middle of a raw autumnal night. He, at least, was practicing upon the maxim laid down by the Archduke Charles, in his principles of strategy, that the commander who wants to give energy to his troops must live with the advanced guard.

But as to Porter on that day, nothing can be made plainer than that from the moment he found one of Rosser's videttes in front of him he gave up every thought of advancing and settled down into absolute inaction. The officers on the skirmish line tell us they found comfort in the understanding that they were "not to bring on an engagement."* General Sturgis, who reported with a brigade just before Porter left the front, was sent back at once to Manassas Junction.† Very soon Sykes' division is found stretched back to Bethlehem Church, and a little later even beyond the forks of the Sudley road, so that General Tower, himself a regular, recognized the regular troops on the right-hand side of the road as he marched in Ricketts' division, past them to the field.‡ Morell's men began soon to follow in the same direction as General Griffin and others tell us,§ till long before dark the whole

---

\* Vol. 2, pp. 660-661. † Vol. 2. p. 689.
‡ Vol. 2, p. 452. § Vol. 1, p. 158.

command, except the skirmishers and one brigade, was strung along the road, expecting momentarily the signal to march to Manassas, and Porter had written his dispatch to McDowell, saying, in substance, that as he was satisfied that Pope had been beaten, whilst he himself was thus lying idle within earshot, he had determined to withdraw.

Porter's counsel wasted a deal of ingenuity in trying to show that he had ordered an advance of some sort before he got the half-past four order. To what end? Is there the slightest indication that any new conjuncture had arisen, or that any new facts had come to Porter's knowledge to make him push at five, when he had lain stock-still since eleven? If his military conscience had by that time become uneasy, it only proves that he knew he ought to have acted long before.

On the Union side, in the morning, the central line was the old Warrenton Ridge road, and the plainly indicated strategic movement for our army was to swing forward a strong left flank, interposing it between Jackson and Longstreet, if possible, before the junction of their forces, the movement being made simultaneously by the whole line, and with as much *ensemble* as possible. If Longstreet had not arrived, the line of battle would have been parallel to the general Confederate line, and a chance in a ranged battle could have been accepted or declined, according to circumstances. Therefore, if Porter had been at the north edge of the woods instead of being in them when the forward move of the morning was made, it is seen at once that he could have gone forward on the left of Reynolds. Now, where would that have taken him? Let us see. The testimony proves beyond cavil that Schenck occupied the woods south of the pike, marked on Warren's map between the words "Warrenton" and "Gainesville" in capitals. Reynolds was on his left, and these two divisions were swinging the left forward to get toward the right flank of Jackson. Had Porter been on their flank there would have been four Union divisions nearly on a line from the woods just spoken of, where Schenck found the dead and wounded, toward the Monroe or Hampton Cole house. That such a line would more than fill the space is proved by the fact that Longstreet filled *what Porter claims* is the same line, with only two divisions, viz: Kemper's and Jones'.

If, therefore, Porter's movement had been coincident in time with Schenck's and Reynolds', he would have come into line whenever he reached the Hampton Cole house in his front, and if, by promptly pressing forward when he came to Dawkins Branch, this would have resulted, we need not care (as I have said in another place) whether it was "by good luck or good management," he could, in fact, have been in his proper place on the field.

We have seen that in Lee's opinion, as an expert, it took Longstreet about two and a half hours to get into position after the head of his column reached the field, and it is, no doubt, a fair estimate. But Porter needed only to have the *head* of his column on the Stuart hill to have had the whole field under his eye. From the Hampton Cole house he could have seen for himself where Schenck and Reynolds were, he would have had straight communication by the Warrenton and Alexandria road along the ridge to Pope's head-quarters, and could have solved by actual vision every question of topography as well as of tactics. To have held that point even for ten minutes would have shown to him how to retire, if he must retire, by a concentric movement, which would have kept him in position relatively to the rest of the army, for the ridge road would have been his own. Even if Longstreet's wing had already been there, a temporary possession of such a point on so important a field was worth a severe struggle. With the information and the orders he already had, and the knowledge of the situation he already possessed, with the noise of his comrades' battle in his ears, and with the conviction which he was too intelligent to lack, that from the bare hill before him he would see what the forest around Morell alone was hiding, it is too plain for serious argument that he ought to have pushed for that hill-top. When we add to this what we have seen of the actual movement of Reynolds and Schenck, whilst he was lying there, and the fact that neither in time nor in place was Longstreet near him, our judgment must go with the Court-martial of 1863, that what he did was a military crime.

When we are told of the newly-discovered evidence, found chiefly in the charitable disposition of Confederate officers to speak kindly of the "bridge that carried them safe over," and to remember things as favorably as possible, and when we are asked in reliance on this to falsify the reports of nearly every National officer on the field, from Meade on the left to Poe on the extreme right, it is well to recall the fact that among this newly-discovered evidence is this, that the total force of our army on that field was superior to Lee's combined army by just about the amount of Porter's corps. The latest historian of that campaign, himself friendly to Porter, gives the number of Heintzelman's, Reno's and McDowell's corps at 53,000 men. Lee's he puts at 54,000, including cavalry.*

The rest were engaged in deadly contest with the

---

* Ropes' Army under Pope, pp. 194–199.

enemy. The orders of General Pope were aimed at thrusting this surplus strength with a telling blow upon the flank of his opponent, or, if you please, upon the extreme right of his line, and we are told it was not safe to do it. In behalf of the soldiery of the American army we may insist that the thing lacking to make it only that danger out of which courage "plucks the flower safety" was the proper leadership for this flanking force; this it was which needed, in the language which Porter had written to Burnside, something "to give it heart if not head." The truth is that its leader lacked heart.

### THE HALF-PAST FOUR ORDER.

At half-past four, Pope, impatient at hearing nothing of Porter, sent his peremptory order to attack at once. The time when this reached Porter has been sharply contested, and a strong and direct attack was made upon the veracity of Captain Douglas Pope, who carried it. To brand this officer as a perjurer has not seemed too great a price to pay for Porter's reinstatement. A careful attention to the evidence shows that this attack is entirely undeserved and is cruelly unjust.

In Warren's written dispatch to Sykes, dated at 5:45 P. M., we have one of those reliable dates, like that of Sykes to Morell in the morning, which must outweigh all mere efforts of memory. Mark that

Griffin's brigade of Morell's division was then a mile and a half or two miles from the front,* which would bring them very near Porter's head-quarters. Warren's brigade of Sykes' division was just east of them. Randol, of the regular artillery, was so close to Porter's head-quarters that he saw Captain Pope arrive, and was soon told that he had "got to go to the front again." † The order went to Morell, he sent back to Griffin, Griffin made his column about face, Warren did the like, and *after that*, he wrote his dispatch to Sykes, with the hour noted above. That all this took half an hour needs no telling, and the testimony proves, beyond reasonable cavil, that it was done in consequence of the order Captain Pope had brought. That order reached Porter, therefore, a very few minutes indeed after five o'clock. Amid all the wild guessing as to hours, which makes it almost ridiculous to rely on what anybody in that command remembers as to time on that day, this dispatch of Warren gives us sure and solid ground of the sort I have tried to make the criterion in the various parts of that day's history. Captain Pope received the order at half-past four, tells us it took him from half to three-quarters of an hour to carry it to Porter. This impregnable array of facts shows that it was delivered

---

\* Vol. 1, p. 158.   † Vol. 2, p. 146.

as he said it was. There can be no satisfaction to any true soldier in the picture of Porter's command that afternoon, and all must wish, for the sake of the common reputation of American arms, that there had been a gleam of energy somewhere in those weary hours. The order to go to the front again was hardly issued before it was recalled; it was too late for Porter to do any thing, but Wilcox, who had been sent to Longstreet's flank in the expectation that Porter might do something, was on his way back to join in the fierce assault it was not too late for the Confederates to make upon McDowell's men at Groveton on the pike.

### PORTER'S DISPATCHES.

If, however, lack of energy were all the fault we had to find with Porter's conduct, it would be comparatively easy to pardon it. It is the reading of his dispatches to McDowell and King which makes it hardest to reconcile his actions with a spirit of honest service to his commander. First of all, we are not permitted to overlook the fact that it was his duty to communicate directly and fully with the General-in-chief on the field. From the time McDowell marched up the Sudley road, Porter was acting under Pope's orders alone, under no obligation to communicate at all with McDowell unless they came into such neighborhood on the field that information might be exchanged for the good of the common cause. The "joint order" had no longer any effect, whatever might have been its original intent. Almost immediately after McDowell left, Porter went back nearly to the forks of the Sudley road, between there and Bethlehem Church, and his tents were pitched between the roads. We are not permitted to forget that this was the direct road from Pope's own position or head-quarters on the field to Manassas Junction, and that as McDowell had expected to leave that road and move into position somewhere on a prolongation of Morell's line, it would be more direct to communicate with Pope than with McDowell, even if there were no imperative duty to do so. It will not do to say he did not know where Pope was. He had staff-officers and orderlies to find him. He did not know where McDowell was, and his staff-officers and orderlies had to find him, and found him, in fact, with General Pope. In the dispatch sent in the morning early, Pope had said he was following the enemy down the Warrenton turnpike. In the joint order he had said his head-quarters would be with Heintzelman or at Centerville, Porter's imperative duty was to communicate with his commander, by seeking him first with Heintzelman's corps, which was fighting near this Sudley road, north of the Warrenton pike, and we know that in sending there, his messenger would have passed Pope's head-quarters on the way. He did nothing of the kind. From daylight till dark no single message is shown to have been sent from him to his commander on the field.

Men who have served in the war do not need to be told that it was not the wont of General officers to report to another subordinate when they could avoid it. Interchange of news or counsel, and requests for assistance and coöperation were common, but any man who has seen service will smile at the idea of Porter's thinking he was under McDowell's command after they had separated, when Pope had never ordered him to report to McDowell, and the only pretended subordination is based upon the provisions of the army regulations whilst both remained together and both were detached from the main army. McDowell went to join that main army, and, of course, Porter knew he was then answerable to the General-in-chief. Porter's dispatches to McDowell, in no sense differ from those exchanged between officers who are independent of each other, but who wish to coöperate. He tells what he means to do, without asking whether McDowell approves or not: does not intimate that he was looking to McDowell for orders; does not imply that he is not also fully in communication with Pope, as it was his primary duty to be.

But the reading of the contents of those dispatches is our most painful task in the light of these facts, and of his actual personal situation close to the Manassas and Sudley road. He says he "failed in getting Morell over to him." This implies an expectation on McDowell's part that this could be done, and a feeling on his own part of the necessity of explanation. The truth, as the evidence shows it, is that McDowell's back was hardly turned before he stopped Morell, the latter having encountered no obstacle worth naming. Not only did he not try to get Morell over, but what we now know of the field shows that there was no difficulty in doing so if he had chosen. Men who have marched through the Wilderness, through the thickets of Northern Georgia where the compass was their constant guide, or through the Salkehatchie swamps, making their dozen or fifteen miles of corduroy road a day, can feel nothing but contempt for the talk of obstacles between Porter and Groveton, where his men could have marched by the flank and his artillery have moved easily behind them on the Five-forks road along that dry and level ridge. From the Manassas Gap Railway on which McDowell and Porter rode, to the head of Compton lane, in the open ground on the other side of the woods, is barely a mile by the scale. But besides all this, the statement was baseless in fact. General Morell testified that no effort whatever, great or small, was made after McDowell left.

"After wandering about in the woods for awhile I withdrew him," the dispatch goes on to say. This means an effort on a large scale—the wandering of a division over a region where there was room for a division to wander. The plain truth is that the division could not have been all deployed to the right without having that flank where it could see out of the woods on the other side, and the simple deployment of the corps could not have been made without being partly in the fields over which Reynolds moved. Take the distance from Morell's position on the Gainesville road to Porter's own head-quarters near the Sudley road, and over which the command remained stretched during that afternoon, and measure with it from Morell northward, and see where it will bring you.

"My scouts could not get through," "my messengers have run into the enemy"—what astounding assertions are these! The road from his own head-quarters by which McDowell had marched to join Pope is known to have been absolutely free from any approach of the enemy, and had been occupied by our troops most, if not all of the day. King's division had passed over it just after noon, and Ricketts' division was marching over it whilst he was writing these words. Parties had been using it carrying rations and ammunition from Manassas to the troops at the front. Porter's dispatches to Morell bear internal evidence of containing information which he got from some of these parties as they passed. What then can be meant by messengers running into the enemy? As for scouts, there is no evidence that one was sent out in any direction. Two artillery officers, seeking water for their horses, rode out through the bushes towards Five-forks and were fired upon by some one whom they did not see, and who was probably a straggler from Reynolds' command, who took them for an enemy. There is positively nothing else in the testimony on which these statements can be based. Stuart's officers, Longstreet, and all of our own who were north of the ridge road, unite in testifying that not even a Confederate skirmish line came east of the Hampton Cole house till late in the day, and it is ridiculous, with the map before us and anybody's marking of the lines, to say there was any thing to prevent a regiment or a squad from going to the north edge of that woods during any half-hour from eleven A. M. of the 29th till the next morning.

But these dispatches could convey to those who might receive them but one impression, and by every rule of interpretation their author must be held to have meant it. They implied that Porter was at Morell's front, earnestly endeavoring to advance, and trying hard to communicate across country with our troops on the north of the woods; that this was his natural and only means of communicating with the rest of the army; and that any communication with Pope, except in this way, was impracticable. In doing this they are given to understand that his forces have been over-matched by the enemy, that his cavalry and his messengers are used up or captured, and that in spite of the most vigorous exertions, isolated and outnumbered, he was forced to decide upon a retreat to Manassas as a matter of manifest necessity. But in this impression, so conveyed, there would not be one word of truth. He was not at the front, but at the rear, where a highway, traveled by our troops and wagons all day long, led directly to Pope's headquarters. He had shown his skirmish line a moment to the enemy and drawn a few distant cannon shots, and had then disappeared so utterly that they reported him gone to take part in the attack upon Jackson. There is no evidence that a man was hurt in his command, and if his messengers were captured, it must have been by our own troops on or near the Sudley road.

In like manner the alarming intelligence he sends, that the enemy was "moving largely" toward his left, purports to be based upon the appearance of the dust, and the reports of scouts. We now know from the Confederate reports that there was no movement toward his left, and that every thing on the Confederate right was kept in a strictly defensive attitude. We know also that there were no "scouts" sent out by him, but only a stationary line of skirmishers under Marshall. The story of any force passing beyond his left was purely the invention of some one's fears, but it was none the less well calculated to discourage Pope, if it should reach him through McDowell. If it was an illusion which anybody honestly held, the vigorous advance of a few regiments in that direction would have dispelled it.

Unless a better explanation of these things can be given than anywhere appears in the record of the Board investigation, we are warranted in saying that these dispatches alone, in connection with the newly-discovered evidence as to the facts, are sufficient to support the original judgment of the Court-martial. The reputation of Porter and his troops before that time was such as to make him responsible for doing what a good officer could do, not what might be expected from a worthless one. It is in view of all these circumstances that the exhibition of motive shown in his letters to Burnside gains double significance, and forces us to the conclusion that his disaffection to Pope had led him beyond the verge of criminal insubordination, and turned what might reasonably be expected to be a triumph of our arms on the 29th of August into the prelude of a disaster on the next day.

To remit the remainder of a continuing punishment by restoring him to citizenship, like other acts of amnesty and oblivion, would be magnanimous. But to vote him a triumph, to record his conduct as the model of chivalry and excellent soldiership, to enrich him from the public treasury, to restore him to his rank, to retire him on pay ten times as great as the pension your maimed and crippled comrades of similar grade in this Society are receiving, is to do dishonor to every one who really threw his soul into the struggle for his country. Whatever may be the social or the clique influences which favor it or bring it about, we have no choice but to protest against it. However honored may be the names which support it, it is our solemn duty to say, under your leadership we did not so learn the art of war. Least of all can we overlook the fact that it was on this very field the Confederate General Jackson extorted the admiration of all soldiers, whether friends or foes, by an audacity, a courage, and an intensity of will and purpose which marked him as a great soldier, and which were the completest contrast, in every particular, with the conduct on which we have commented.

# APPENDIX.

### I. PORTER'S LETTERS TO BURNSIDE—EXTRACTS.

FROM WARRENTON JUNCTION, *August* 27, 1862.—4 P. M.
GENERAL BURNSIDE, *Falmouth, Va.*:

I send you the last order from General Pope, which indicates the future as well as the present. Wagons are rolling along rapidly to the rear, as if a mighty power was propelling them. I can see no cause of alarm, though this may cause it. McDowell is moving to Gainesville, where Sigel now is. The latter got to Buckland bridge in time to put out the fire and kick the enemy, who is pursuing his route unmolested to the Shenandoah, or Loudoun County. . .

Every thing has moved up north. I found a vast differance between these troops and ours, but I suppose they were new, as to-day they burned their clothes, etc., when there was not the least cause. I hear that they are much demoralized, and needed some good troops to give them heart, and, I think, head. We are working now to get behind Bull Run, and I presume will be there in a few days, if strategy don't use us up. The strategy is magnificent, and tactics in the inverse proportion. I would like some of my ambulances. I would like also to be ordered to return to Fredericksburg, to push toward Hanover, or with a larger force to push toward Orange Court-house. I wish Sumner was at Washington, and up near the Monocacy, with good batteries. I do not doubt the enemy have a large amount of supplies provided for them, and believe they have a contempt for the Army of Virginia. I wish myself away from it, with all our old Army of the Potomac, and so do our companions. . .

There is no fear of an enemy crossing the Rappahannock. The cavalry are all in the advance of the rebel army. . .

Most of this is private, but if you can get me away, please do so. Make what use of this you choose, so it does good. Don't let the alarm here disturb you. If you had a good force you could go to Richmond. A force should be at once pushed on to Manassas to open the road. Our provisions are very short. F. J. PORTER.

---

WARRENTON, 27.—P. M.

To GENERAL BURNSIDE:

Morell left his medicine, ammunition and baggage at Kelly's ford. Can you have it hauled to Fredericksburg and stored? His wagons were all sent to you for grain and ammunition. I have sent back to you every man of the First and Sixth New York Cavalry, except what has been sent to Gainesville. I will get them to you after awhile. Every thing here is at sixes and sevens, and I find I am to take care of myself in every respect. Our line of communications has taken care of itself in compliance with orders. The army has not three days' provisions. The enemy captured all Pope's and other clothing; and from McDowell the same, including liquors. No guard accompanying the trains, and small ones guard bridges. The wagons are rolling on, and I shall be here to-morrow. Good night.

F. J. PORTER, Major-General

## APPENDIX. 75

Four Miles from Manassas, 28th.—2 p. m.

Major-General Burnside:

All that talk about bagging Jackson, etc., was bosh. That enormous gap, Manassas, was left open and the enemy jumped through; and the story of McDowell having cut off Longstreet had no foundation. The enemy has destroyed all our bridges, burned trains, etc., and made this army rush back to look at its line of communication, and find us bare of subsistence. We are far from Alexandria, considering the means of transportation. Your supply train of forty wagons is here, but I can't find them. There is a report that Jackson is at Centerville, which you can believe or not. The enemy destroyed an immense amount of property at Manassas, cars and supplies. I expect the next thing will be a raid on our rear, by way of Warrenton pike, by Longstreet, who was cut off. F. J. Porter, Major-General.

Bristow—6 a. m. 29th

Major-General Burnside:

I shall be off in half an hour. The messenger who brought this says the enemy had been at Centerville, and pickets were found there last night. Sigel had a severe fight last night; took many prisoners. Banks is at Warrenton Junction; McDowell near Gainesville; Heintzelman and Reno at Centerville, where they marched yesterday; and Pope went to Centerville, with the last two as a body-guard, at the time not knowing where was the enemy, and when Sigel was fighting within eight miles of him and in sight. Comment is unnecessary.

The enormous trains are still rolling on, many animals not being watered for fifty hours. I shall be out of provisions to-morrow night. Your train of forty wagons can not be found. I hope Mac's at work and we shall soon be ordered out of this. It would seem, from proper statements of the enemy, that he was wandering around loose, but I expect they know what they are doing, which is more than any one here or anywhere knows. F. J. PORTER, Major-General.

### 2. POPE'S ORDERS TO PORTER.

HEAD-QUARTERS ARMY OF VIRGINIA,
BRISTOW STATION, *August* 27, 1862—6:30. P. M.

GENERAL:

The Major-General Commanding directs that you start at one o'clock to-night, and come forward with your whole corps, or such part of it as is with you, so as to be here by daylight to-morrow morning Hooker has had a very severe action with the enemy, with a loss of about three hundred killed and wounded. The enemy has been driven back, but is retiring along the railroad. We must drive him from Manassas and clear the country between that place and Gainesville, where McDowell is. If Morell has not joined you, send word to him to push forward immediately. Also send word to Banks to hurry forward with all speed to take your place at Warrenton Junction. It is necessary on all accounts that you should be here by daylight. I send an officer with this dispatch who will conduct you to this place. Be sure to send word to Banks, who is on the road from Fayetteville, probably in the direction of Bealeton. Say to Banks, also, that he had best run back the railroad trains to this side of Cedar Run. If he is not with you, write him to that effect.

By command of MAJOR-GENERAL POPE.

GEORGE D. RUGGLES, Colonel and Chief of Staff.
MAJOR-GENERAL F. J. PORTER, Warrenton Junction.

P. S.—If Banks is not at Warrenton Junction, leave a regiment of infantry and two pieces of artillery as a guard till he comes up, with instructions to follow you immediately. If Banks is not at the Junction, instruct Colonel Clary to run the trains back to this side of Cedar Run, and post a regiment and section of artillery with it.

By command of MAJOR-GENERAL POPE.

GEORGE D. RUGGLES, Colonel and Chief of Staff.

---

HEAD-QUARTERS ARMY OF VIRGINIA,
NEAR BULL RUN, *August* 29, 1862.—3 A M.

GENERAL:

McDowell has intercepted the retreat of Jackson; Sigel is immediately on the right of McDowell; Kearney and Hooker march to attack the enemy's rear at early dawn. Major-Gen. Pope directs you to move upon Centerville at the first dawn of day with your whole command, leaving your trains to follow. It is very important that you should be here at a very early hour in the morning. A severe engagement is likely to take place and your presence is necessary. I am, General, very respectfully,

Your obedient Servant,

GEORGE D. RUGGLES, Colonel and Chief of Staff.

MAJOR-GENERAL PORTER.

---

HEAD-QUARTERS ARMY OF VIRGINIA,
CENTERVILLE, *August* 29, 1862.

MAJOR-GENERAL PORTER:

Push forward with your corps and King's division, which you will take with you, upon Gainesville. I am following the enemy down the Warrenton turnpike. Be expeditious or we will lose much. JOHN POPE,

Major-General Commanding.

HEAD-QUARTERS ARMY OF VIRGINIA,
CENTERVILLE, *August* 29, 1862.

GENERALS MCDOWELL AND PORTER:

You will please move forward with your joint commands toward Gainesville. I sent General Porter written orders to that effect an hour and a half ago. Heintzelman, Sigel and Reno are moving on the Warrenton turnpike, and must now be not far from Gainesville. I desire that as soon as communication is established between this force and your own, the whole command shall halt. It may be necessary to fall back behind Bull Run at Centerville to-night. I presume it will be so on account of our supplies. I have sent no orders of any description to Ricketts, and none to interfere in any way with the movements of McDowell's troops, except what I sent by his aide-de-camp last night, which were to hold his position on the Warrenton pike until the troops from here should fall upon the enemy's flank and rear. I do not even know Ricketts' position, as I have not been able to find out where General McDowell was until a late hour this morning. General McDowell will take immediate steps to communicate with General Ricketts, and instruct him to rejoin the other divisions of his corps as soon as practicable. If any considerable advantages are to be gained by departing from this order, it will not be strictly carried out. One thing must be held in view, the troops must occupy a position from which they can reach Bull Run to-night or by morning. The indications are that the whole force of the enemy is moving in this direction at a pace that will bring them here by to-morrow night or next day. My own head-quarters will be, for the present, with Heintzelman's corps, or at this place.

JOHN POPE, Major-General Commanding.

APPENDIX. 79

HEAD-QUARTERS IN THE FIELD,
*August* 29, 1862. 4:30, P. M.

Your line of march brings you in on the enemy's right flank. I desire you to push forward into action at once on the enemy's flank, and, if possible, on his rear, keeping your right in communication with General Reynolds. The enemy is massed in the woods in front of us, but he can be shelled out as soon as you engage their flank. Keep heavy reserves and use your batteries, keeping well closed to your right all the time. In case you are obliged to fall back, do so to your right and rear, so as to keep you in close communication with the right wing.

JOHN POPE, Major-General Commanding.
TO MAJOR-GENERAL PORTER.

---

HEAD-QUARTERS ARMY OF VIRGINIA,
IN THE FIELD NEAR BULL RUN, *August* 29, 1862. 8:50 P.M.

GENERAL:

Immediately upon receipt of this order, the precise hour of receiving which you will acknowledge, you will march your command to the field of battle of to-day, and report to me in person for orders. You are to understand that you are expected to comply strictly with this order, and to be present on the field within three hours after its reception or after day-break to-morrow morning.

JOHN POPE, Major-General Commanding.
MAJOR-GENERAL F. J. PORTER.

---

3. PORTER'S DISPATCHES TO MCDOWELL.

GENERALS MCDOWELL OR KING:

I have been wandering over the woods, and failed to get

a communication to you. Tell how matters go with you. The enemy is in strong force in front of me, and I wish to know your designs for to-night. If left to me I shall have to retire for food and water, which I can not get here. How goes the battle? It seems to go to our rear. The enemy are getting to our left.

F. J. PORTER, Major-General Volunteers.

GENERALS MCDOWELL & KING:

I found it impossible to communicate by crossing the woods to Groveton. The enemy are in force on this road, and as they appear to have driven our forces back, the fire of the enemy having advanced, and ours retired, I have determined to withdraw to Manassas. I have attempted to communicate with McDowell and Sigel, but my messengers have run into the enemy. They have gathered artillery and cavalry and infantry, and the advancing masses of dust show the enemy coming in force. I am now going to the head of the column to see what is passing and how affairs are going, and I will communicate with you. Had you not better send your train back.

F. J. PORTER, Major-General.

GENERAL MCDOWELL:

Failed in getting Morell over to you. After wandering about the woods for a time, I withdrew him, and, while doing so, artillery opened upon us. My scouts could not get through. Each one found the enemy between us, and I believe some have been captured. Infantry are also in front. I am trying to get a battery, but have not succeeded as yet. From the masses of dust on our left, and from reports of scouts, think the enemy are moving largely in that way.

APPENDIX. 81

Please communicate this way this messenger came. I have no cavalry or messengers now. Please let me know your designs, whether you retire or not. I can not get water, and am out of provisions. Have lost a few men from infantry firing. F. J. PORTER, Major-General Volunteers.
*Aug.* 29, 6 P. M.

### 4. DISPATCHES OF OTHER OFFICERS.

*August* 29, 1862. 8:30 *o'clock.*
GENERAL MORELL:

General Porter desires you to keep closed up and see that the ammunition train, which is, I learn, at Manassas, is put in with our train. Yours respectfully,
GEORGE SYKES.

*Endorsed.* MANASSAS JUNCTION.
GENERAL:

There is an ammunition train here belonging to King's division; nothing for us.
GEORGE W. MORELL, Major-General.
To MAJOR-GENERAL PORTER.

HEAD-QUARTERS CAVALRY BRIGADE. 9:30 A. M.

Seventeen regiments, one battery and five hundred cavalry passed through Gainesville three quarters of an hour ago, on the Centerville road. I think this division should join our forces now engaged at once. Please forward this.
JOHN BUFORD, Brigadier-General.
To GENERAL RICKETTS.

5*h.* 45*m.* P. M., *Aug.* 29, '62.
GENERAL SYKES:

I received an order from Mr. Cutting to advance and support Morell. I faced about and did so. I soon met

6

Griffin's brigade withdrawing by order of General Morell, who was not pushed out, but returning. I faced about and marched back two hundred yards or so. I then met an orderly from General Porter to General Morell, saying he must push on and press the enemy; that all was going well for us, and he was returning. Griffin then faced about, and I am following him to support General Morell, as ordered. None of the batteries are closed up to me.

Respectfully,<br>
G. K. WARREN.

## DISPATCHES BETWEEN PORTER AND MORELL.*
(VOL. 2, PP. 26–27.)

### I.

GENERAL: Colonel Marshall reports that two batteries have come down in the woods on our right, toward the railroad, and two regiments of infantry on the road. If this be so, it will be hot here in the morning.

GEO. W. MORELL, Major-General.

To GENERAL PORTER.

(This was returned to Morell endorsed as follows:)

### II.

Move the infantry and everything behind the crest and conceal the guns. We must hold that place and make it too hot for them. Come the same game over them they do over us, and get your men out of sight.

F. J. PORTER.

---

\* Col. Marshall's testimony on page 115 fixes the time of his information to Morell, which must have preceded all these, as between three and four P. M.

### III.

GENERAL PORTER: I can move everything out of sight but Hazlitt's battery. Griffin is supporting it, and is on its right, principally in the pine bushes. The other batteries and brigades are retired out of sight. Is this what you mean by every thing?

GEO. W. MORELL, Major-General.

(Indorsed as follows:)

### IV.

GENERAL MORELL: I think you can move Hazlitt's battery, or the most of it, and post him in the bushes with the others, so as to deceive. I would get every thing, if possible, in ambuscade. All goes well with the other troops.

F. J. P.

### V.

GENERAL MORELL: Tell me what is passing, quickly. If the enemy is coming, hold to him, and I will come up. Post your men to repulse him.

F. J. PORTER, Major-General.

### VI.

GENERAL MORELL: Push over to the aid of Sigel, and strike in his rear. If you reach a road up which King is moving, and he has got ahead of you, let him pass; but see if you can not give help to Sigel. If you find him retiring move back toward Manassas, and should necessity require it, and you do not hear from me, push to Centerville. If you find the direct road filled, take the one *via* Union Mills, which is to the right as you return.

F. J. PORTER, Major-General.

Look to the points of the compass for Manassas.

## VII.

General Morell: Hold on, if you can, to your present place. What is passing? F. J. Porter.

## VIII.

General Porter: Colonel Marshall reports a movement in front of his left. I think we had better retire. No infantry in sight, and I am continuing the movement.

Stay where you are, to aid me if necessary. Morell.

## IX.

General Morell: I have all within reach of you. I wish you to give the enemy a good shelling without wasting ammunition, and push at the same time a party over to see what is going on. We can not retire while McDowell holds his own. F. J. P.

## X.

General Morell: I wish you to push up two regiments supported by others, preceded by skirmishers, the regiments at intervals of 200 yards, and attack the section of artillery opposed to you. The battle works well on our right, and the enemy are said to be retiring up the pike. Give the enemy a good shelling as our troops advance.

F. J. Porter, Major-General Commanding.

## XI.

General Morell: Put your men in position to remain during the night, and have out your pickets. Put them so that they will be in position to resist any thing. I am about a mile from you. McDowell says all goes well, and we are getting the best of the fight. I wish you would send me a dozen men from that cavalry.

F. J. PORTER, Major-General.

Keep me informed. Troops are passing up to Gainesville, pushing the enemy. Ricketts' has gone, also King.*

---

### 5. REPORTS OF U. S. OFFICERS—EXTRACTS.

MAJOR-GENREAL HEINTZELMAN:

"At 10 A. M. I reached the field of battle, a mile from Stone Bridge on the Warrenton Turnpike. General Kearney's division had proceeded to the right and front. I learned that General Sigel was in command of the troops then engaged. At 11 A. M. the head of Hooker's division arrived. General Reno an hour later. . . . . . .

The firing continued some time after dark, and when it ceased, we remained in possession of the battle-field."

BRIGADIER-GENERAL SCHENCK. (*He being disabled by a wound, his report was made by Colonel Cheesebrough, his Adjutant-General.*)

"It was at this time, one or two o'clock, that a line of skirmishers were observed approaching us from the rear, they proved to be of General Reynolds. We communicated with General Reynolds at once, who took his position on our left, and at General Schenck's suggestion he sent a battery to our right in the woods for the purpose of flanking the enemy. They secured a position, and were engaged with him about an hour, but with what result we were not informed. Gen-

---

\* The order of these dispatches is that in which they were arranged by General Morell in his testimony. None of them have the hour noted upon them.

eral Reynolds now sent us word that he had discovered the enemy bearing down upon his left in heavy columns, and that he intended to fall back to the first woods behind the cleared space, and had already put his troops in motion. We therefore accommodated ourselves to his movement."

BRIGADIER-GENERAL REYNOLDS. (*Supplemental report referring to Colonel Cheesebrough.*)

"I sent no word to General Schenck of the kind indicated in this paper of the movement of the enemy at the time this change of position was made, nor at any time. There was a report came later in the evening that the enemy were moving over the pike, but I am not aware that I communicated it to General Schenck, as at that time I had no connection with him."

COLONEL CHEESEBROUGH. (*Explanatory of foregoing.*)

"General Reynolds did not communicate directly with General Schenck, as it would appear from my report, but the information was received through Colonel McLean who told General Schenck that General Reynolds had informed him that 'the enemy was bearing down, etc., and that he (Reynolds) intended to fall back, and has actually commenced the movement.' Colonel McLean wished to know if he should act accordingly. General Schenck directed him to accommodate himself to General Reynolds' movements."

---

6. REPORTS OF CONFEDERATE OFFICERS—EXTRACTS.

GENERAL R. E. LEE. *Official Report.*

"Longstreet entered the turnpike near Gainesville, and moving down toward Groveton, the head of his column came upon the field in rear of the enemy's left, which had already opened with artillery upon Jackson's right, as previously described. He immediately placed some of his batteries in position, but before he could complete dispositions to attack, the enemy withdrew; not, however, without loss from our artillery. Longstreet took position on the right of Jackson, Hood's two brigades, supported by Evans, being deployed across the turnpike, and at right angles to it. These troops were supported on the left by three brigades under General Wilcox, and by a like force on the right under General Kemper. D. R. Jones' division formed the extreme right of the line, resting on the Manasses Gap Railroad. The cavalry guarded our right and left flanks, that on the right being under General Stuart in person. After the arrival of Longstreet, the enemy changed his position, and began to concentrate opposite Jackson's left, opening a brisk artillery fire, which was responded to with effect by some of General A. P. Hill's batteries. Colonel Walton placed a part of his artillery upon a commanding position between Generals Jackson and Longstreet, by order of the latter, and engaged the enemy vigorously for several hours.

"Soon afterwards General Stuart reported the approach of a large force from the direction of Bristow Station, threatening Longstreet's right. The brigades under General Wilcox were sent to re-enforce General Jones, but no serious attack was made, and after firing a few shots the enemy withdrew. While this demonstration was being made on our right, a large force advanced to assail the left of Jackson's position, occupied by the division of General A. P. Hill. The attack was received by his troops with their accustomed steadiness, and the battle raged with great fury. . . . . .

"While the battle was raging on Jackson's left, General Longstreet ordered Hood and Evans to advance, but before the order could be obeyed, Hood was himself attacked, and his command at once became warmly engaged. General Wilcox was recalled from the right and ordered to advance on Hood's left, and one of Kemper's brigades, under Colonel Hunton, moved forward on his right."

GENERAL JAMES LONGSTREET. *Official Report.*

"On approaching the field some of Brig.-Gen. Hood's batteries were ordered into position, and his division was deployed on the right and left of the turnpike, at right angles with it, and supported by Brig.-Gen. Evans' brigade. Before these batteries could open, the enemy discovered our movements, and withdrew his left. Another battery, Captain Stribling's, was placed upon a commanding position to my right, which played upon the rear of the enemy's left, and drove him entirely from that part of the field. He changed his front rapidly so as to meet the advance of Hood and Evans. Their brigades, under General Wilcox, were thrown forward to the support of the left, and three others, under General Kemper, to the support of the right of those commands. Gen. D. R. Jones' division was placed upon the Manassas Gap Railroad to the right and in echelon with regard to the three last brigades. Colonel Walton placed his batteries in a commanding position between my line and that of General Jackson, and engaged the enemy for several hours in a severe and successful artillery duel. At a late hour in the day, Major-General Stuart reported the approach of the enemy in heavy columns against my extreme right. I withdrew General Wilcox with his three brigades, from the left, and placed his command in a position to support Jones in case of an attack against my right. After some few shots the enemy withdrew his forces, moving them around toward his front, and about four o'clock in the afternoon began to press forward against General Jackson's position. Wilcox's brigades were moved back to their former position, and Hood's two brigades, supported by Evans, were quickly pressed forward to the attack. At the same time Wilcox's three brigades made a like advance, as also Hunton's brigade of Kemper's command."

GENERAL A. P. HILL. *Official Report.*

"Friday morning, in accordance with orders from General Jackson, I occupied the line of the unfinished railroad, my extreme left resting near Sudley's Ford; my right near the point where the road strikes the open field. . . . . . .

"The evident intention of the enemy this day was to turn our left and overwhelm Jackson's corps before Longstreet came up; and to accomplish this, the most persistent and furious onsets were made by column after column of infantry, accompanied by numerous batteries of artillery. Soon my reserves were all in, and up to six o'clock my division, assisted by the Louisiana brigade of General Hays, commanded by Colonel Forno, with an heroic courage and obstinacy almost beyond parallel, had met and repulsed six distinct and separate assaults, a portion of the time the majority of the men being without a cartridge."

GENERAL J. E. B. STUART. *Official Report.*

"The next morning (29th) in pursuance of General Jackson's wishes, I set out again to endeavor to establish communications with Longstreet, from whom he had received a favorable report the night before. Just after leaving the Sudley road, my party was fired on from the wood bordering the road, which was in rear of Jackson's lines, and which the enemy had penetrated with a small force, it was afterward ascertained, and captured some stragglers. They were between General Jackson and his baggage, at Sudley.

I met with the head of General Longstreets column between Haymarket and Gainesville, and then communicated to the Commanding General, General Jackson's position and the enemy's. I then passed the cavalry through the column so as to place it on Longstreet's right flank, and advanced directly toward Manassas, while the column kept directly down the pike to join General Jackson's right. I selected a fine position for a battery on the right, and one having been sent to me, I fired a few shots at the enemy's supposed position which induced him to shift his position.

General Robertson, who, with his command, was sent to reconnoiter further down the road toward Manassas, reported the enemy in his front. Upon repairing to that front, I found that Rosser's regiment was engaged with the enemy to the left of the road, and Robertson's videttes had found the enemy approaching from the direction of Bristow station toward Sudley. The prolongation of his line of march would have passed through my position, which was a very fine one for artillery as well as observation, and struck Longstreet in flank. I waited his approach long enough to ascertain that there was at least an army corps, at the same time keeping detachments of cavalry dragging brush down the road from the direction of Gainesville, so as to deceive the enemy (a ruse which Porter's report shows was successful), and notified the Commanding General, then opposite me on the turnpike, that Longstreet's flank and rear were seriously threatened, and of the importance to us of the ridge I then held. Immediately upon the receipt of that intelligence, Jenkins', Kemper's and D. R. Jones' brigades and several pieces of artillery were ordered to me by General Longstreet, and, being placed in position fronting Bristow, awaited the enemy's advance. After exchanging a few shots with rifled pieces, this corps withdrew toward Manassas, leaving artillery and supports to hold the position till night."

GENERAL J. E. B. STUART. *Memoranda made part of his report.*

"Friday, August 29th. As General Stuart rode forward, toward Groveton, about ten o'clock A. M., he found the enemy's sharpshooters had penetrated the woods, going toward the ambulances and train, threatening to cut them off. He at once directed Captain Pelham, of the Stuart Horse Artillery, who was near by, to shell the woods, and gather up all the stragglers around the train and drive back the enemy, notifying General Jackson in the meantime of what was transpiring. . . . . . . . . . .

" General Stuart also sent Colonel Baylor, who was near the railroad embankment, in command of the Stonewall brigade, etc. . . . . Having ordered Captain Pelham to report to General Jackson, General Stuart went toward Haymarket to establish communication with Generals Lee and Longstreet, accompanied by Brigadier-General Robertson, with a portion of his, and a portion of General F. Lee's cavalry."

GENERAL JUBAL A. EARLY (of Jackson's command), *Official Report.*

" Early next morning (August 29th), the division was formed on a ridge perpendicular to the railroad track, with the right resting on the Warrenton turnpike and facing toward Groveton. In a short time thereafter, I received an order from General Jackson to move, with my own and Hays' brigade, to a ridge west of the turnpike and the railroad track, so as to prevent the enemy from flanking our forces on the right, a movement from the direction of Manassas indicating that purpose having been observed.
When this corps (Longstreets) had advanced sufficiently far to render it unnecessary for me to remain longer in my position, or for the Thirteenth and Thirty-first regiments to re-

main where they were, I recalled them and moved to the left for the purpose of rejoining the rest of the division.

"I found General Lawton, with his brigade, in the woods, not far from the position at which I had been the evening before, but formed in line so as to be parallel to the railroad, Trimble's brigade being posted on the railroad cut, on the right of our line as thus contracted. I was ordered by General Lawton to form my brigade in line in rear of his brigade, and Colonel Forno was directed to form on my right.

"Shortly after this the enemy began his attempts to drive our troops from the line of the railroad, and about half-past three, P. M., Colonel Forno was ordered to advance to the front by General Jackson, to the support of one of General A. P. Hill's brigades."

GENERAL C. M. WILCOX. *Official Report.*

"Hopewell Gap is about three miles from Thoroughfare Gap, being connected with the latter on the east by two roads, one of which is impracticable for wagons. The enemy had been at this pass during the day, but retired before night, thus giving us a free passage. Early the following morning our march was resumed, and the command rejoined at half-past nine A. M., the remainder of the division at the intersection of the two roads leading from the gaps above mentioned.

Pursuing our line of march together with the division, we passed by Gainesville and, advancing some three miles beyond, my three brigades were formed in line of battle on the left and at right angles to the turnpike. Having advanced near three-quarters of a mile, we were then halted. The enemy was in our front and not far distant. Several of our batteries were placed in position on a commanding eminence to the left of the turnpike A cannonading ensued, and continued for an hour or two, to which the enemy's artillery replied

"At half-past four or five P. M., the three brigades were moved across to the right of the turnpike, a mile or more, to the Manassas Gap Railroad. While here musketry was heard to our left, on the turnpike. This firing continued with more or less vivacity till sundown. Now the command was ordered back to the turnpike, and forward on this to the support of General Hood, who had become engaged with the enemy and had driven him back some distance, inflicting severe loss upon him, being checked in his successes by the darkness of the night."

MAJOR S. H. HAIRSTON, (Stuart's cavalry). *Official Report.*

GAINESVILLE, *August* 29, 1862, 8 P. M.

"To COLONEL CHILTON, Assistant Adjutant-General:

"In obedience to General Lee's order I started this morning at eight o'clock with one hundred and fifty cavalry to go to Warrenton, 'to find out if any of the enemy's forces were still in the vicinity of that place.' I went from Thoroughfare to the right on a by-road, which took me into the Winchester road two miles below Warrenton, and came up to the rear of the town. I inquired of the citizens and persons I met on the way, but could not hear that any of their forces were in the vicinity of that place. They informed me that the last left yesterday in the direction of Gainesville and Warrenton Junction."

## 7. ORAL TESTIMONY.

PASSAGES REFERRED TO IN THE TEXT. EXTRACTS.

W. L. B. WHEELER (Citizen). *Record, Vol.* 3, *pp.* 1109-11.

*Q.* Did Bethlehem church have a spire on it on the 29th of August, 1862? *A.* It never has had since I have known it. *Q.* How long have you known it? *A.* I suppose I have known it since I was eight years old. I went to school there in 1834. . . . . .

*Q.* Relative to Bethlehem church, when did the walls fall in of that structure? *A.* I could not say when, because I did not see it until the spring of 1862. I did not even know that of my own knowledge, but I understood that the Southern soldiers had taken the inside woodwork in building their winter-quarters. *Q.* When did it fall in? *A.* During the winter. *Q.* During the winter of 1862? *A.* Yes. I can not say the exact month or week that they commenced taking timbers from the house. It was a very old frame building.

JOHN T. LEACHMAN (Citizen). *Record, Vol.* 3, *pp.* 1115–6.

*Q.* I did not recollect whether you testified about Bethlehem church on your former examination? *A.* I did not; I do not think. *Q.* Did Bethlehem church ever have a spire to it? *A.* No, sir. *Q.* Or a belfry? *A.* No, sir. . . . *Q.* Of what material was it? *A.* The house was built of brick. . . . . .

*Q.* What is that hill at Monroe's called? *A.* I never heard it called any thing but Monroe's hill, until since the war I have heard it called frequently Stuart's Hill. *Q.* How long after the war did you hear it called that? *A.* Really, I could not say; very frequently. I reckon that very soon after the war it was called Stuart's Hill. *Q.* Never heard a reason ascribed for it? *A.* Yes, I did. I heard that Stuart was on that hill during the 29th, and I think the family of Monroe, from that circumstance, called it Stuart's Hill. It is a short distance from Monroe's house."

GENERAL ORLANDO M. POE (U. S. Engineers). *Vol.* 2, *pp.* 579–80.

" We formed between the Matthews house and the road—

our left resting on the road—formed in line of battle and moved directly forward, our left touching the road, toward Bull Run, nearly due north. We continued that movement until we crossed Bull Run, or at least a portion of the brigade; two regiments did not cross; advanced some distance to the north of Bull Run, two or three hundred yards, perhaps; and after perhaps an hour there, we were recalled. Or at least from the time that we got across until we got back, was perhaps an hour. . . *Q.* What was your position at that time in reference to the rest of General Pope's army? *A.* The extreme right flank, so far as I know; the right flank of the infantry, certainly. . . . . *Q.* What time do you fix it to have been in the morning that that artillery opened on you when in that advanced position? *A.* About eleven o'clock, I should think. I assume it at that; I did not look at my watch. *Q.* Nearer ten or nearer twelve? *A.* I should say about eleven. That is an estimate I made some years ago and put in writing at that time. I see no reason to change it.

GENERAL SAMUEL P. HEINTZELMAN, *Commanding Third Army Corps. Vol. 2, p. 604.*

*Q.* Did you keep a diary of events that transpired? *A.* Yes, I carried a memorandum book in my pocket, and I made a note of every thing that was brought to me that I supposed would be of use to me in making my reports. *Q.* When did you make these notes? *A.* On the spot, during the day.

(Extracts from diary read) . . . At ten A. M. reached the field, a mile from the Stone Bridge. Firing going on, and I called upon General Sigel. General Kearney was at the right. Part of General Hooker's division I sent to support some of Sigel's troops. General Hooker got up about

11 A. M. General Reno nearly an hour later. Soon after General Pope arrived—about quarter to two. I rode to the old Bull Run battle-field where my troops were. The enemy we drove back in the direction of Sudley Church, and they are now making another stand. We are hoping for McDowell and Porter."

COLONEL SAMUEL N. BENJAMIN, *Assistant Adjutant-General, United States Army. Vol. 2, pp. 606-608.*

Q. What rank did you hold and command on the 29th of August, 1862? A. I was first lieutenant in the Second United States Artillery, in command of battery E. . . I got into action, as near as I can recollect, a little after twelve o'clock; but I can not be very certain of the hour. Q. With what command were you on duty at that time? A. I went up there with Stevens' division,* and before I got into action I was ordered to report to Sigel; I reported to General Schenck. I am not sure that I saw General Sigel at all. . . . I went to my battery, and got it on the road, and brought it back and put it in position on the ridge, just this side of Groveton, about 200 yards from the house. . . Soon after that the enemy opened fire upon me; they lay on a ridge. I did not see any of their men to the left of the pike, but on the right, according to my recollection, there were eighteen guns, ranging from 1,000 to 1,100 yards, about 1,500 yards from me. . Q. About what time did you take that position? A. As near as I can recollect, half-past twelve. Q. At that time every thing was very still? A. Very still at the time I got up there. I had heard firing before. Q. How long did it remain still? A. About an hour or more, then I got engaged myself. Q. How long did

---

*Stevens' division was in Reno's ninth corps.

you remain at that point? *A.* I must have remained at that point over three hours; then I went on the road to near the Stone house. I had suffered very heavily in men and material, and I re-organized my battery.

GENERAL ROBERT C. SCHENCK, *Commanding Division Sigel's Corps. Vol.* 3, *pp.* 1008, 1012.

*Q.* Where was that (your) division early on the morning of that day, August 29th. *A.* We were upon the hills below Bull Run, up in the neighborhood of Young's Creek.
*Q.* What formation was your division in? *A.* I had Stahel's brigade upon the right, and McLean's brigade to the left, moving along south of and parallel to the turnpike.
*Q.* At what time of day did you reach your farthest point in advance? *A.* I think it must have been somewhere about the middle of the day, perhaps a little earlier than the middle of the day. *Q.* Did you see General Reynolds' division during that day? *A.* No, but I understood he was off on my left. *Q.* Did you see General Reynolds himself during the morning or afternoon? *A.* No, I think not; I don't recollect.
*Q.* How far did you get beyond the Gibbon woods, in which the wounded of the night before were? *A.* I don't know that we got beyond the Gibbon woods. My remembrance is that the farthest point we reached was somewhere about the west edge of the Gibbon wood—that is, the wood in which Gibbon's troops were engaged the night before. We found there his wounded, and the evidence of the battle that had taken place. *Q.* At what time did you quit, with your division, this Gibbon wood? *A.* I should think, to the best of my recollection, somewhere between one and three o'clock. I don't think I can be more positive than that. My recollection is that it was sometime after noon. *Q.* To what point did you then go with your division?

*A.* In consequence of reports made to me in reference to the movements of General Reynolds, I thought it best for me to fall back, and I came into a strip of woods which I suppose to be these. (South of the 'ville' in 'Gainesville' on Warren's map.) I formed in line of battle near the west edge of that woods. There we lay most of the afternoon. . . .
*Q.* With reference to your advanced point, where were you at the time Benjamin was placed where his batteries were? *A.* That I can not tell. *Q.* Have you any recollection as to whether you were then in Gibbon's wood? *A.* I do not recollect. My impression, rather, is that I was not at that time in Gibbon's wood. *Q.* How long after Benjamin being placed in that position do you think that you reached Gibbon's wood? *A.* I can not tell you. *Q.* How long after that opening fire began with such severity upon Benjamin? *A.* After he was placed there. *Q.* Yes? *A.* I think he had occupied the position for some little time. Perhaps half an hour or more. He was firing an occasional shot before the enemy seemed to discover his range and position, and concentrated their fire upon him.

General N. C. McLean, *Colonel Commanding Brigade Schenck's Division. Vol. 2, pp. 883, 884.*

*Q.* Where were you on that morning (29th)? *A.* On the battle-field of Bull Run. *Q.* What time did you go into action? *A.* We were ordered quite early in the day, as I supposed at the time on the extreme left of our troops; we advanced toward the position of the enemy in line of battle, with a very heavy line of skirmishers, the skirmishers engaged more or less as we advanced, sometimes severely, sometimes very lightly, but the opposition to us was not so heavy as to prevent our advance. We advanced slowly and regularly; that was the condition of affairs. We halted at times

## APPENDIX. 99

to examine the position, and then went on again until the afternoon. Quite late in the afternoon we were ordered back into camp. During the day, exactly at what portion of the day I can not now state, General Meade came to me, and said he was ordered to take position on our left; he was in General Reynolds' division. General Meade was commanding the brigade. *Q.* George D. Meade? *A.* Yes; afterward Commander of the Army of the Potomac. I halted and he came up with his troops; we then went on, and he took position on our left. Some time afterward—the intervals of time I can not give you at all, regulated more by events than time then—General Meade came back with his brigade, saying to me that he had placed a battery, and he had been shelled out of his position by the rebel batteries, and had got into a hornet's nest of batteries; he was then coming back and advised me to do the same. I reported to General Schenck, my division commander, the facts, and in a short time we were ordered back a little distance, and remained there until night-fall. . . *Q.* How far do you suppose you advanced forward? *A.* I can not give you an estimate; we were in line of battle the whole time, from the time we moved early in the morning. We moved along for some time before we found any reply to our skirmishers; then it was continuous dropping fire; sometimes it was very severe, and sometimes not severe. We kept advancing very slowly; occasionally we would halt and skirmish along to find out where we were, and what the enemy were doing, and then advance again. That was kept up all the day until in the afternoon, when General Meade came back; we did not advance any more after that.

GENERAL JOHN F. REYNOLDS (Commanding division McDowell's corps), *Vol.* 1, *p.* 166.

*Q.* Do you, or not, know where the enemy's right flank was on the afternoon of the 29th, say towards sunset. *A.* I was on the extreme left of our troops facing the enemy, and their right towards sunset had been extended across the pike, with fresh troops coming down the Warrenton turnpike. But up to twelve or one o'clock it was not across the pike, and I had myself made an attack on their right with my division, but was obliged to change front to meet the enemy coming down the Warrenton pike. I was forming my troops parallel to the pike, to attack the enemy's right, which was on the other side of the pike, but was obliged to change from front to rear on the right, to face the troops coming down the turnpike. That was, I suppose, as late as one o'clock, and they continued to come in there until they formed and extended across the turnpike. . . . *Q.* Did you see any of the enemy's forces on the 29th, on the south of the pike leading from Gainesville to Groveton, and do you not know that the right of the enemy's line rested on the north of that road? *A.* Their line changed during the day. I was on their right up to twelve o'clock, or about that time. In the afternoon it was extended across the pike. I can not state how far; the country was very wooded there, and I could not see how far across it was. I thought at the time, they were extending it that afternoon until dark. . .

*Q.* On the 29th of August, did or did not the enemy's right outflank your left at any time? *A.* I think it did towards evening. It was late, not dark, towards the dusk of the evening. . . *Q.* Did the enemy outflank you at sunset of the 29th? *A.* My division, with a brigade of Sigel's corps, lost connection for a time with the remainder of Sigel's corps, but at sunset we had closed in to the right, so that the enemy, I

APPENDIX.    101

think, did outflank us at sunset. That is, I think his flank extended beyond ours, although distant from us; not near enough to be engaged.

COLONEL THOMAS L. ROSSER (Confederate in Stuart's cavalry), *Vol.* 3, *p.* 1073.

*Q.* Did you join General Stuart that morning (29th); if so, state at what time and narrate what happened. *A.* At daylight I moved out, crossing the Alexandria and Warrenton turnpike, and occupied a road leading off to Manassas Junction, a mile or two beyond the turnpike. At this point, about ten o'clock, I was joined by General Stuart and his staff. Longstreet's command was coming in in a very forced and disordered march from the direction of Thoroughfare Gap, moving rapidly and straggling badly. My position was taken up with reference to their protection from a gun of the enemy, who were in my front. When Stuart joined me he notified me that the enemy was moving on our right flank, and orderd me to move my command up and down the dusty road, and to drag brush, and thus create a heavy dust as though troops were in motion. I kept this up at least four or five hours.

MAJOR B. S. WHITE (Confederate on General Stuart's staff), *Vol.* 3, *pp.* 983-991.

*Q.* Where were you on the morning of Friday, August 29th, 1862? *A.* Near Sudley church. *Q.* Do you know any thing that transpired in your immediate vicinity on that morning? If so, what was it? *A.* On that morning we were looking south; there were some troops appeared on our left, Federal troops, and there was some little confusion in our ambulance train just north of Sudley Springs. *Q.* What then transpired? *A.* There were some artillery and troops put in position to open on the enemy in *that* direction (wit-

ness indicated that the artillery was west of Sudley church) firing east across Bull Run. *Q.* Do you know whose battery that was that was put in position? *A.* Pelham's battery; he commanded the Stuart horse artillery. *Q.* What then transpired? *A.* Major Patrick was ordered to charge, and did charge the enemy in that direction and lost his life there. . *Q.* Then what was the next event that transpired? *A.* We moved off across the country to find out what had become of Longstreet's corps; we moved off in this way, toward Thoroughfare Gap. *Q.* Did you find General Longstreet's columns or corps advancing? *A.* We did, between Haymarket and Gainesville. *Q.* What did General Stuart then do? *A.* General Stuart then threw his command on Longstreet's right, and moved down with his right flank in the direction of Bristow and Manassas Junction. . . . We took the road leading directly down the Manassas Gap railroad; there is a road running parallel with it. . . . General Stuart threw his command on the right of Longstreet, and passed down the Manassas Gap railroad to about that point (west of Hampton Cole's, point marked *W*). . .
We discovered a column in our front, discovered a force in our front coming from the direction of Manassas Junction to Bristow. . . . It was a good point for observation; a high position, elevated ground. We could see Thoroughfare Gap and Gainesville, and all the surrounding country. . . . *Q.* What did General Stuart then do? *A.* He put a battery in position on that hill. . . My instructions were to put a battery in position there, and open on the column advancing in this direction. His instructions to me were to go to General Jackson and report the fact of this column moving in that direction. . . I went across *here* (parallel to Pageland Lane). General Jackson's corps was *here*; that is, his command was along the Independent

Manassas Gap Railroad*, and the batteries were posted right on a range of hills in the rear of that. I found General Jackson on a range of hills just in rear of his battery. . . I then started to return to General Stuart. . . I tried to take a little short cut going back to him. I made a little detour. I passed where there had been a skirmish the evening before

Q. Did you find any dead and wounded there? A. I did.
Q. North of the pike or south of the pike? A. On the north side. Q. Did you find General Stuart at once? A. It was some time before I found him; a half or three-quarters of an hour. Did you halt on the way going back? A. I passed a little time with General Jackson after I reported to him, because the batteries were engaged; his batteries were on Stony Ridge. His line of battle was along the Independent line of the Manassas Gap Railroad; there was a battery that came out about the point of that woods (just northwest of the Matthew's house and west of the Sudley pike); just about that point there was a battery from the Union side that came out there and took position, and I stayed there some time watching the artillery duel between the guns stationed here and that battery. Then going back to General Stuart I took a little short cut and passed over some ground where there had been a fight the evening before, and there were some dead on the field. In going back I met a cousin of mine who commanded a battalion connected with Ewell's corps, which was engaged in this fight; he was reconnoitering; I went along with him and saw what was in my front. I suppose it was half or three-quarters of an hour before I got back to General Stuart. . . Q. When you got

---

*. This is the unfinished railroad, not the Manassas Gap Railroad, into which its line ran.

back to General Stuart, where was he? *A*. Where I left him, on that hill. *Q*. At that time where was General Longstreet's command? *A*. They had come down and were forming *here*. (Witness indicates a point back, west of Pageland Lane). . . . *Q*. What became of this column of troops that you saw advancing? *A*. I don't know what became of them. They disappeared from our front. *Q*. Do you know of any other position being taken up by General Longstreet's command, during the day, in advance of the position that you have indicated; if so, when and where? You indicated a position back of Pageland Lane. *A*. I do not. *Q*. How long were you down in the neighborhood of this hill which you have marked with a cross, during that day? up to what time? *A*. We were down there the greater part of the day; we were on the extreme right all the time afterwards. The cavalry remained on the extreme right until the morning of the 30th. *Q*. Do you know of any other measures taken to retard the advance of this column of troops from the direction of Manassas Junction or Bristow, that day by General Stuart, other than the planting of that battery in that position? *A*. I do not. Before that battery was put in position, Robertson's brigade of cavalry and Rosser were engaging the enemy in our front. When that battery was put in position and opened on the enemy, it checked them and they retired. Then General Stuart told me to go to General Jackson and report the fact that this column was advancing in this direction. *Q*. During that day what sort of an action was going on on the 29th, to your knowledge? *A*. There was very heavy fighting going on up here in Jackson's front. . . . *Q*. What time do you think you met General Longstreet between Haymarket and Gainesville? *A*. It was about eleven o'clock. *Q*. Was General Longstreet at the head of his column? *A*. He was near the head of the column. . . . *Q.* How long a conversation did General Stuart have with General Lee or General Longstreet? *A.* Ten or fifteen minutes. . . . . . *Q.* How long was it before you arrived at the front marked W, by you on this map. *A.* It could not have been over three-quarters of an hour or an hour. . . . *Q.* Were those troops (Porter's) near any house that you could see? *A.* They were near the Carraco house. *Q.* Very near? *A.* Perhaps a little beyond. *Q* Did not you see any troops in the direction of the place marked " Lewis-Leachman house," on that day? *A.* Yes, there were troops there, too.* *Q.* How were they disposed? Are you certain that no shots were fired from that direction at the men about in the neighborhood of the Lewis-Leachman house? *A.* No, I am not certain, though I believe that there were. *Q.* Are you not certain that most of the shots were fired in that direction? *A.* I am unable to answer that for this reason: at the time that battery was put in *there,* firing in this direction upon the Manassas Gap Railroad, General Stuart requested that I should go *here,* and report the fact to General Jackson, which I did; I went off then and was gone at least three-quarters of an hour or an hour. . . . *Q.* What time do you put it that you came back from General Jackson after being sent over by General Stuart? *A.* Half-past two or three o'clock.

REV. JOHN LANDSTREET, (Chaplain Confederate Army,)
    *Vol.* 3, *pp.* 996–1003.

*Q.* Where were you on the morning of August 29th, 1862? *A.* I was between Sudley Springs and Aldie, about midway in the mountain. *Q.* Did you join General Stuart that day. *A.* I joined him for the first time for eight

---

* This was the position from which Reynolds advanced.

months, after our Catlett Station raid. I think I reached Sudley between eight and nine in the morning. *Q.* Was General Stuart there? *A.* Yes, sir. *Q.* Do you recollect any circumstance transpiring after you arrived there? *A.* No, sir. Just before we arrived there was a little confusion or kind of stampede among the baggage train. I don't know that I noticed any of our cavalry there unless it was those connected with the commissary's and quarter-master's department. But there was a little skirmish there about that time which attracted my attention. . . . *Q.* Do you know at what time you left Sudley? *A.* No, sir: I recollect that the next place where I was, was called Cole's. It was an elevated position, rather in the angle between Gainesville and Bristow. . . . *Q.* At what time in the day were you at Hampton Cole's? *A.* I did not have a watch, but I think it was somewhere toward ten o'clock in the day. *Q.* What did you see there which has impressed itself upon your attention? *A.* There was considerable dust in *this* direction, indicating a body of troops. . . . General Stuart ordered some of the Fifth Cavalry to go and cut brush and drag it along the road. . . *Q.* Who was the Colonel of that regiment? *A.* T. L. Rosser—we frequently after that conversed about it. . . There was some firing from this position in the direction of this approaching force. . . *Q.* What became of this column of troops upon those shots being fired? *A.* I did not see them. *Q.* They disappeared from your sight? *A.* Yes, sir. *Q.* Where did General Longstreet form his command? (In answer the witness marked upon the official map a position west of Pageland Lane). *Q.* What time of day was that that they were all in position? *A.* When I say that, I say so simply from my recollection and guessing at the time. Mr. Maltby (counsel for Porter)—Then I object if he guesses.

## APPENDIX. 107

The Witness.—What I guess is this: Every man has a way of forming an idea of an hour of the day based upon his experience. It is my recollection that it was somewhere between two and three o'clock. . . *Q.* How late in the day do you recollect seeing General Hood's division? *A.* Between three and four o'clock. *Q.* Where was it then? *A.* Where I have indicated on the map.

LEWIS B. CARRACO, *citizen, Vol.* 2, *pp.* 921-923.

"*Q.* Where did you reside on the 29th August, 1862? *A.* Where I now reside, very near the Manassas Gap Railroad. *Q.* Were you there that day? *A.* I was. *Q.* Up to what hour in the day did you remain there? *A.* I was there until very late Friday evening. *Q.* During the day did you see any Confederate forces? If so, when? *A.* I saw some cavalry scouts during the day, and in the evening there was a battery firing some seventy-five or eighty yards back of my house, just west of my house, and an officer came there and told me I was in danger, and to take my family and go back of the line. *Q.* Where did you go? *A.* I went up the road about a mile, to a farm owned now by Major Nutt.

*Q.* Toward Gainesville? *Q.* Between there and Gainesville. *Q.* Did you meet any Confederate force on that trip? If so, about where? *A.* I saw them a little beyond Hampton Cole's; a very small number. They were sitting down on the side of the railroad, and their battery that was planted at the back of my house, that opened on the Federal troops directly after I passed it; and when I got up there against them, they got up and took shelter on the embankment of the railroad. *Q.* Did you at that time see any troops to the south of the railroad? *A.* None at all except a little picket force that was a little to the south of the railroad just above there; a small picket force. *Q.* Did any Confederate force pass to the east of your house during the day? If so, in what direction did they go? *A.* I saw none pass to the eastward. I saw some shelling from the back of what is called the Britt farm,* and a disabled Federal wagon at the mouth of a lane, called Compton's Lane. *Q.* About what time in the day was that? *A.* I could hardly say. Twelve or one o'clock. *Q.* You say in the evening you saw a battery west of your house? *A.* I think it was only one cannon, seventy-five or eighty yards from the house. *Q.* What do you mean by the expression "evening"? *A.* I mean something like three or four o'clock; somewhere thereabouts. . . *Q.* What time was the cannon posted there? *A.* Possibly, four o'clock. *Q.* You are positive about that? *A.* I am not positive; but according to the best of my judgment it was probably as late as four. *Q.* Was it earlier or later than four? *A.* It was not earlier, I do not think; not earlier than three, I am very sure. . . . . *Q.* Were there any soldiers of any description about your house, except the battery? *A.* On Friday there was a Federal force in Mr. Lewis's field, to the east of my house. *Q.* Where was Lewis's field. *A.* Within 300 or 400 yards to the east of my house.

WILLIAM THOMAS MONROE (Citizen), *Vol.* 2, *p.* 924.

*Q.* Where were you residing on the 29th of August 1862? *A.* At home (place on the Monroe Hill designated on the map). *Q.* Is there any considerable elevation near your residence? If so, where is it? *A.* There is, just here. (Witness indicates.) *Q.* What do you call that hill? *A.* We never had any name for it at all, until since the war, when it has got the name of Stuart's Hill; I don't know how, unless it was that there was a battery of Stuart's on that hill during Friday of the fight. *Q.* In August? *A.* Yes, the 29th

---

* This farm is between Cole's and the turnpike.

of August, 1862. Q. From that hill what points can be seen? A. Manassas and Centerville. Q. How as to the Bull Run range of mountains? A. You can see the mountains very plainly. Q. Do you recollect any thing of the occurrences on the 29th of August, 1862? A. I recollect about eleven o'clock General Longstreet's troops first came in then, or about twelve; I reckon that battery was posted on that hill; it may have been a little earlier, but not later than twelve o'clock. Q. Do you know in what direction that battery was fired? A. It fired in the direction of Groveton. Q. Did it continue to fire in that direction? A. It fired in that direction some hours, or may be more. Q. Do you know where it went to from that point? A. It went down by, just into the depot that is now upon the railroad, and from there to the hill at the Britt house. . .
. . Q. Do you know where the Confederate lines were, or forces, on that day, aside from that particular battery that finally got down to the Britt house? A. There was infantry just in *here*, running from the Warrenton and Gainesville pike (back of Pageland Lane.) There was an army road running through there, and there they were posted on this road, (witness marks the map). Q. Do you know how far down they were posted? A. I don't know. (Witness closes his marking at the road just west of Charles Randall's.) The skirmish line was drawn down as far as Vessel's. Q. When did you first see the Confederate lines advance beyond Pageland Lane during the day—the infantry? A. I don't know when *this* part of the line advanced at all (down near the railroad). It moved down under the hill out of sight of the house. I did not see them. Q. Off in what direction? A. Off in *this* way, I suppose. (In the direction of Hampton Cole's.) Q. Down along the railroad, do you say? A. They moved in that direction, down along the railroad. Q. About what

time of day was it? *A.* I think it was about the middle of the afternoon, say three or four o'clock. *Q.* You were describing some portion of the line that you *did* see? *A.* This portion of the line marched through by the house— that was about three o'clock. (The line just north of the house.) *Q.* That portion of the line between your house and the turnpike, you mean? *A.* Yes, sir. *Q.* Marched to the front about four o'clock? *A.* I think it was General Hunton's brigade. General Hunton was along with the brigade, and I thought he was commanding. *Q.* Do you know of the advance of any of the other Confederate forces that day, during the day? *A.* I do not. *Q.* Did you remain there during the day, in that vicinity? *A.* I was about the house and about on the farm during that day. I do not recollect leaving the farm at any time. . . *Q.* Did you see any separate body of men after the advance of the first line marched across by your house? *A.* I did not see any marching to the place at all on Friday, except this brigade that I took to be Gen. Hunton's. *Q.* Could you see from your house to Hampton Cole's? *A.* Very plainly. *Q.* Could you see any lines of troops that would be formed along what is called Meadowville Lane?* *A.* I did not see any troops at all formed along Meadowville Lane, but about some time between three and four o'clock there were some Confederate troops formed right along here in the woods (south of Hampton Cole's), I think one regiment.

COLONEL WILLIAM W. BLACKFORD, (Confederate, Stuart's staff), *Vol.* 2, *p.* 672.

*Q.* Which direction did you take in going to meet

---

* This lane runs from Hampton Cole's northward to the turnpike, and is the position on which Porter claims that Longstreet's line was formed.

Longstreet that morning? *A.* I do not recollect whether we followed the Warrenton turnpike, or whether we cut across fields; I am inclined to think we cut across; I think we did not follow the turnpike. The enemy were in strong force, and I think we avoided the turnpike, so as to strike across the country. We had a detachment of cavalry with us, and when we got in sight of Longstreet's dust, we galloped ahead to meet the column. *Q.* Where was that, relative to the position of Gainesville and Haymarket? *A.* It was beyond Gainesville; I do not recollect how far. . . *Q.* How long should you say, from your recollection, General Stuart and General Lee halted for their conversation? *A.* They just waited there till the cavalry could have gotten across; I should suppose within a quarter of an hour. . . *Q.* Where did General Stuart go? *A.* Then we galloped across to our right. . . *Q.* Where were you during the day after you left this place near Monroe's? *A.* I was all around *here* (Young's Branch) reconnoitering. *Q.* From the direction of Lewis-Leachman's? *A.* Yes; all around that quarter— Britt's and Hampton Cole's. *Q.* Do you know of any movement, during the day, of the corps that was on this Manassas and Gainesville road, beyond Dawkins Branch? *A.* No, sir. *Q.* Was your position such that it would have fallen under your observation if there had been such a movement? *A.* I think we would have been sent over there if there had been. . .
*Q.* In going towards General Lee in the morning, why did you not take the pike as your line of march? *A.* I do not know exactly why. This road from Gainesville goes off at a considerable angle towards Thoroughfare Gap. I suppose General Stuart struck across *here*. I do not recollect that he told me his object; but I recollect that we were not on that pike. We had met videttes, and we expected to run into

scouting parties all the time. I know there were a good many turns in the road, and we were a little nervous at the small force that was with us, and a little uneasy that we would not be able to make the connection. *Q.* Were you afraid that scouts might be around in that country? *A.* Yes; we thought very likely the enemy would get in in force, and have cavalry bodies out there. *Q.* Did you see at any time during the day a body of men in the ravine in the neighborhood of Cunliffe's, marked Meadowville on the map— Union troops? *A.* I do not understand the question. *Q.* Did you see a large force, a brigade or two brigades, in the neighborhood of Cunliffe's, in a ravine, at any time during the day, or in the ravine near the word "Meadowville" about five o'clock in the afternoon of the 29th, or four o'clock, or three o'clock? *A.* I do not recollect seeing them. *Q.* Do you recollect whether the Confederate lines included that or not at that time? *A.* Longstreet's first line was back of that; I think his first line was in *these* woods (west of Pageland Lane). *Q.* Do you say that from positive knowledge? *A.* No, sir; I do not know exactly; that was his first line after he first deployed. *Q.* How soon did he advance? *A.* I do not know.

COLONEL E. G. MARSHALL, *Thirteenth New York Volunteers, and Captain of Regulars.* *Vol.* 2, *pp.* 130–132.

*Q.* Where were you on the afternoon of the 29th August last? *A.* I was on the road leading to Gainesville—the road from Manassas Junction. *Q.* On what duty? *A.* On duty with General Morell's division in General Porter's corps, and commanding my regiment. *Q.* Specify the character of duty you were performing that afternoon? *A.* About one o'clock I was detailed by General Porter to go with my regiment across an open country and ravine to some timber that

was facing our line of battle, and deploy skirmishers to find out the position of the enemy, and any thing else that I could find out concerning them. *Q.* State the position and force of the enemy in the immediate vicinity of General Porter's command, as far as you know it. *A.* Immediately after going there, my skirmishers were fired on by a body of dragoons, and shortly afterward there was a section of artillery which opened fire upon General Porter's command. Soon after that, perhaps about two o'clock, the head of a large column came to my front. They deployed their skirmishers and met mine, and about three o'clock drove my skirmishers into the edge of the timber. We were all on the left of the Manassas road, going towards Gainesville. Their force continued to come down all day; in fact, until one o'clock at night. It was a very large force, and they were drawn up in line of battle as they came down. I reported at different intervals to General Morell, my immediate commander, the position of the enemy. But at one time I deemed it so important that I did not dare to trust orderlies or others with messages, and I went myself up to him to confer concerning the enemy. This was about dusk. General Morell told me that he had just received orders from General Porter to attack the enemy, to commence the attack with four regiments. . . About the same time, before I went in to General Morell, I could hear and judge of the result of the fighting between the force of the enemy and General Pope's army. I could see General Pope's left and the enemy's right during the greater part of the day, about two miles off, perhaps more, diagonally to our front and to the right. The enemy set up their cheering, and appeared to be charging and driving us, so that not a man of my command but what was certain that General Pope's army was being driven from the field. Afterward, at dark,
8

I was sent for by General Porter, and questioned very stringently with reference to the enemy, and my remarks to him were the same as I am now making, and as I made to General Morell. . . . . (The witness read as follows, being No. 34 of the printed statement of the petitioner.)

"GENERAL MORELL: The enemy must be in much larger force than I can see. From the commands of the officers, I should judge a brigade. They are endeavoring to come in on our left, and are advancing. Have also heard the noise on left as the movement of artillery. Their advance is quite close.

"E. G. MARSHALL, Colonel Thirteenth New York."

*Q.* Was that written before or after you crawled out? *A.* That was written before, upon the reports received from different parts of my skirmish line. . . . . After this dispatch was gotten off, I then went with Major Hyland of the Thirteenth New York, and was conducted by him to a certain open space on the front of my picket line; from this map I suppose it was somewhere in this vicinity (northwest of Randall's);* crawling out some distance, so that I could look beyond this point of timber (if it is correct on this map) north-west, in this direction, perhaps a mile, I discovered a force, the right of which was resting on a timber that jutted on our front. Major Hyland had been there preceding me, and stated that the line went only a little distance beyond, and it was unsafe to go further. . . . . I accepted his statement, and concluded it was best to return to headquarters, and report the state of affairs; that the enemy was drawn up in line of battle, in full view, and were infantry, and the line was a parallel to my position that I was occupy-

---

\* Randall's house, on the official map, was a short distance south of Cole's. A mile north-west from those points the infantry were first seen by him, west of Pageland Lane.

ing that day.* I returned to my head-quarters, and made another more positive report. . . This force I speak of on the left was developed perhaps about three o'clock. It might have been about three and one half or four that I went out there. Between three and four o'clock I sent the first dispatch. It must have been four o'clock, if not later, when I sent my second dispatch.

GENERAL GEORGE W. MORELL, *Commanding Division in Porter's Corps. Vol.* 1 *p.* 141.

When the head of my division had crossed the railroad at Manassas I was halted, and in a short time received orders to go to Gainesville. As we countermarched to go there, my division was thrown in front, General Sykes having already passed on towards Centerville. We had gone up the road towards Gainesville, perhaps about three miles, when I met a mounted man coming toward us. I stopped him and asked him the road to Gainesville, and also the news from the front. He said that he had just come from Gainesville, and that the enemy's skirmishers were then there to the number of about four hundred, and the main body was not far behind them. I then moved on up the road, and in a short time our own skirmishers reported that they had discovered the enemy's skirmishers in their front. The column was then halted by General Porter, who was with me. After a little consultation he directed the batteries to be posted on the crest of a ridge that we had just passed, and the men to be placed in position. Immediately went about that work. After a while I saw General McDowell and General Porter riding together. They passed off to our right into the woods towards the railroad. After a time General Porter returned; and, I think, alone, and gave me orders to move my com-

---

* Marshall's line was south of Randall's house.

mand to the right over the railroad. I started them, and got one brigade, and I think one battery over the railroad, passing through a clearing (a corn field), and had got to the edge of the woods on the other side of it, when I received orders to return to my former position. I led the men back, and as the head of the column was in front of Hazlitt's battery, which had been put in position, we received a shot from the enemy's artillery directly in front of us. I got the infantry back of the batteries, under cover of the bushes and the crest of the ridge, and posted Waterman's battery on the opposite side of the Gainesville road, and we remained in that position the most of the day. . . . . A little before sunset, just about sunset, I received an order in pencil from General Porter to make dispositions to attack the enemy. That order spoke of the enemy as retiring. I knew that could not be the case from the reports I had received, and also from the sounds of the firing. I immediately sent back word to General Porter that the order must have been given under a misapprehension, but at the same time I began to make dispositions to make the attack in case it was to be made.

Colonel Locke soon after came to me with an order from General Porter to make the attack. I told him (and I think in my message to General Porter I spoke of the lateness of the day) that we could not do it before dark. Before I got the men in position to make the attack, the order was countermanded, and I was directed to remain where I was during the night. General Porter himself came up in a very few minutes afterwards, and remained with me for some time. It was then just in the gray of evening between dusk and dark. . . . . *Q.* About what hour of the day did you first hear musketry firing in force and volume? *A.* There were a few shots exchanged between our pickets and those of the enemy when we first came upon that ground, and a

few scattering shots during the day. With that exception I did not hear any until the volleys I have just spoken of.\*
. . . I am satisfied, upon reflection, that the order of the 29th to attack was not countermanded prior to the receipt of the order to pass the night where I was. I construed the order to pass the night there as being virtually a countermand of the order to attack. I was making dispositions to pass the night when General Porter joined me.

*Vol.* 2, *p.* 442: I suppose, from the nature of the woods which we examined that morning, that we could not get in from that quarter. *Q.* Do you know of any effort to go through that woods? *A.* Nothing further than the inspection made by these two officers that morning.† *Q.* Do you know any thing about those woods? *A.* I don't know any thing about these woods; I have not been there since. The wood was thick, but I did not know any thing about the country. . . *Q.* After those few shots in the morning were there any shots fired by Hazlitt's battery during the day? *A.* No, sir; nothing to fire at that we could see. *Q.* So in point of fact there was nothing going on where you were during the day except those few shots in the morning? *A.* That was all. We were then on the defensive, as I supposed; not ready to attack, certainly. *Q.* On page 350, dispatch No. 28, please state when you received that dispatch on the 29th of August? *A.* "Push over to the aid of Sigel?" I can not designate the hour. *Q.* What efforts did you make to do that? *A.* I did not make any efforts. I must have received almost immediately afterward the order that I read just now, to hold on.

---

\* These were described as in the direction of the rest of Pope's command, "a considerable distance on our right," and "just at the close of day."

† McDowell and Porter when they rode off together to the right.

## APPENDIX.

GENERAL S. D. STURGIS, *Commanding Division, Vol. 2, pp.* 688–689.

*Q.* What rank and command did you hold on the 29th August, 1862? *A.* I was Brigadier-General of Volunteers. I had on that day only one brigade of a division, the principal part of which was back at Alexandria. . . . General Piatt's brigade. . . . *Q.* To whom were you ordered to report? *A.* General Porter—ordered by General Porter himself to join him; that order I received at Warrenton Junction. *Q.* Where did you find General Porter's column? *A.* I found it on the road leading from Manassas Junction in the direction of Gainesville; I should think a mile and a half, about, beyond Bethlehem church. . . *Q.* What did you do? *A.* I reported to General Porter. I rode in advance of my brigade. I found troops occupying the road, and I got up as near as I could get, and then halted my command, and then rode forward to tell General Porter that they were there. He said, For the present let them lie there. *Q.* What did you then do individually? *A.* Well, I simply looked about to see what I could see. I was a stranger to the lay of the land and the troops, and all that; so, without getting off my horse, I rode about from place to place watching the skirmishers, and among other things I took a glass and looked in the direction of the woods, about a mile beyond, which seemed to be the object of attention—beyond the skirmishers. There I saw a glint of light on a gun, and I remarked to General Porter that I thought they were probably putting a battery in position at that place, for I thought I had seen a gun. . He thought I was mistaken about it, but I was not mistaken, because it opened in a moment; at least, a few shots were fired from that place; four, as I recollect. *Q.* What force of the enemy did you see in that direction at that time? *A.* I didn't see any of the enemy at all. *Q.* Then what did you do? *A.* Then, when they had fired, as near as I can recollect, about four shots from this piece, General Porter beckoned to me; I rode up to him and he directed me to take my command to Manassas Junction, and take up a defensive position, inasmuch as the fire seemed to be receding on our right. *Q.* What firing do you mean? *A.* I mean the cannonading that had been going on for some time on our right, probably in the direction of Groveton. . . . *Q.* What time was it when you received that order? *A.* I have no way of fixing the time of day. I have carried in my mind the impression that it was more about the middle of the day—about one o'clock.

## 8. GENERAL GARFIELD'S OPINION IN 1880.

In view of all the peculiar circumstances, and of his relations to the original judgment of the Court-martial, it can not be improper to have on permanent record the evidence that General Garfield saw nothing in the new matter before the Advisory Board to change the conclusions he had deliberately reached in 1863.

"HOUSE OF REPRESENTATIVES, }
WASHINGTON, D. C., *February* 18, 1880. }

MY DEAR COX—In our twenty-five years of acquaintance and friendship, you have never done a greater service to the truth, or given me so valuable a help, as in your letter of the 14th inst., which I have just received. I have been so stung by the decision of the Schofield Board that it is very hard to trust my own mind to speak of it as it appeared to me. I have made a strong effort to separate myself from the case, and to look at it intellectually as though it related only to the pieces on a chess-board, and not to living men, or men who had ever lived; and all my best efforts have brought me out precisely to the conclusions of your letter.

Still, I had not yet made, in the light of the new testimony, a careful strategic study of the field and map as you have done. But how curious it is that what you say now, with the new maps before you, is the exact picture of the field, and Porter's conduct upon it, which glowed in strong colors in my mind, and the mind of the Court-martial, seventeen years ago.

With kindest regards, I am, as ever, yours,

J. A. GARFIELD."

# INDEX.

Archduke Charles of Austria, 57.
Army, Lee's, its strength, 61.
Army, Pope's, its strength, 61.
Banks, Gen. N. P., 33, 41, 76, 77.
Batteries, National:
  Benjamin's, 21, 96.
  Hazlitt's, 83, 116, 117.
  Randol's, 63.
  Waterman's, 116.
Batteries, Confederate:
  Pelham's, 91, 102.
  Stribling's, 88.
  Of Jackson's corps, 103.
  Of Longstreet's corps, 87.
  Walton's battalion, 87.
Baylor, Colonel, 91.
Benjamin, Capt. Samuel N., 21, 22, 24, 98; testimony, 96.
Bethlehem Church, 15, 16, 57, 65, 93, 94.
Blackford, Col. W. W., 42; testimony, 110.
Board, Advisory, its members, 4.
Broad Run, 36.
Bristow, 8, 9, 33, 36, 40, 41, 75, 87, 90, 102, 104.
Britt farm, 108, 109, 111.
Buck Hill, 33.
Buford, Gen. John, 20, 81.
Buford, Gen. N. B., 3, 20.
Bull Run, 13, 17, 78, 79, 95.
Burnside, Gen. Ambrose, 10, 13, 62, 71, 73.

Carraco, L. B., 43, 54, 105; testimony, 107.
Casey, Gen. Silas, 3.
Catharpin Valley, 18, 36, 37.
Centerville, 13, 41, 65, 75, 77, 78, 109.
Cheesebrough, Col. Wm. H., 23, 85, 86.
Chilton, Colonel R. H., 93.
Chinn House, 33.
Clary, Col. Robert E., 77.
Cole House, Hampton, 20, 26, 27, 32, 34, 45, 41, 42, 43, 45, 47, 54, 59, 60, 69, 102, 106, 107, 109, 110, 111.
Compte de Paris, 54.
Compton Lane, 34, 67, 108.
Court Martial of 1862, its members, 3, 50.
Cundliffe House, 23, 49.
Dawkins Branch, 16, 27, 30, 50, 51, 52, 53, 59.
Douglass House, 19, 21, 35, 36, 37, 39.
Drayton, Gen. Thos. F., 47.
Early, Gen. Jubal A., official report, 91.
Evans, Gen. N. G., 87, 88, 89.
Ewell, Gen. R. S., 103.
Five Forks, 67, 69.
Forno, Col. H., 89, 92.
Forrest, Gen. N. B., 56
Fox, Capt. George B., 22.
Franklin, battle of, 56.
Gainesville, 18, 19, 28, 33, 35, 40, 43, 51, 52, 59, 73, 77, 85, 86, 92, 100, 102, 104, 107, 111, 115, 118.

(121)

Garfield, Gen. James A., his relations to the case, 1, 2; member of court martial, 3, 5; opinion, in 1880, 119.
Getty, Gen. George W., member of advisory board, 4.
Gibbon, Gen. John, 22, 23, 26, 30.
Gibbon woods, 22, 23, 27, 37, 97.
Grant, Gen. U. S., 4.
Griffin, Gen. Charles, 57, 82, 83.
Groveton, 4, 21, 34, 53, 64, 67, 96, 100, 109.
Hairston, Maj. Samuel H., 40; report, 93.
Hayes, Gen. Rutherford B., 4.
Haymarket, 18, 19, 24, 28, 38, 91, 102, 104, 111.
Hays, Gen. H. S., 89, 91.
Heintzelman, Gen. Samuel P., 17, 18, 21, 41, 61, 65, 75, 78; report, 85; testimony, 95.
Hill, Gen. A. P., 87; official report, 89, 92.
Hitchcock, Gen. E. A., 3.
Hood, Gen. J. B., 19, 20, 42, 43, 46, 50, 87, 88, 93, 107.
Hooker, Gen. Joseph, 8, 9, 12, 76, 85, 95.
Hopewell Gap., 92.
Hunter, Gen. David, 3.
Hunton, Col. Eppa, 43, 88, 89, 110.
Hyland, Major G., jr., 114.
Jackson, Gen. Thomas J., 12, 17, 19, 22, 23, 24, 25, 26, 27, 36, 46, 58, 59, 70, 72, 77, 87, 89, 102, 103; his position, 37, 38, 41, 42.
Jenkins, Gen. M., 90.
Jones, Gen. D. R., 47, 59, 87, 88, 90.
Kearney, Gen. Philip, 17, 77, 85, 95.
Kemper, Gen. J. L., 47, 50, 59, 87, 88, 90.
King, Gen. Rufus, 3, 41, 52, 64, 68, 80.
Landstreet, Chaplain J., 26, 33, 42; testimony, 105.
Law, Col. E. M., 46.
Lawton, Gen. A. R., 92.
Lee, Gen. Fitzhugh, 91.
Lee, Gen. Robert E., 3, 12, 19, 25, 39, 39, 40, 48, 49, 60, 86, 105, 111; his letter, 28; his position, 46; official report, 86.
Lewis–Leachman House, 37, 49, 105, 111.
Locke, Col. F. T., 116.
Longstreet, Gen. James, met by Stuart, 18, 19, 20; time of his arrival, 20, 22-29, 48, 104, 106, 107; position on the field, 30-39, 43, 45, 104, 106, 112; on the skirmish line, 56; statements compared, 48, 50; official report, 88; other mention, 58, 59, 60, 69, 75, 87, 89, 90, 91, 101.
Manassas Gap Railroad, 36, 37, 67, 87, 88, 93, 105, 107.
Manassas Junction, 39, 40, 51, 57, 65, 67, 79, 70, 75, 80, 90, 102, 104, 112, 118.
Marshall, Col. E. G., 16, 44, 45, 67, 71, 82, 84; testimony, 112.
Matthews House, 17, 94, 103.
McDowell, Gen. Irvin, 16, 33, 43, 46, 58, 64, 65, 66, 67, 68, 69, 71, 73, 75, 77, 78, 84, 115; the joint order, 52, 53, 78.
McLean, Col. Nathaniel C., 22, 24, 86; testimony, 98.
Meade, Gen. George G., 22, 23, 39, 61, 99.
Meadowville Lane, 110, 112.
Monroe, W. T., 42, 43; testimony, 108.
Monroe Hill, 20, 23, 26, 33, 34, 38, 39, 45, 48, 59, 94, 108.
Morell, Gen. George W., 15, 16, 32, 33, 34, 51, 57, 63, 65, 67, 68, 69, 81-85, 113; testimony, 115
Page-land Lane, 30, 38, 42, 45, 50, 102, 104, 106, 109, 112.
Patrick, Major, 102.
Poe, Gen. Orlando M., 17, 18, 28, 61; testimony, 94.

# INDEX.

Pone, Mount, 33.
Pope, Capt. Douglass, 15, 62, 63.
Pope, Gen. John, commanding at second battle Bull Run, 4; animus of Porter toward Pope, 7; order to Porter, August 27, 8, 76; headquarters on 28th, 13; position when Jackson's movements began, 39; position on August 29, 40; his forces, 61; order of 4:30 P. M., 62, 79; order of 8:50 P. M., 79; other orders to Porter, 76-79; headquarters on the field, 65; connection with Porter's headquarters, 70; the fighting with Jackson, 89, 92, 113; other mention, 39, 40, 62, 65, 66.
Porter, Gen. Fitz John, judgment of court martial, 1, 3; correspondence with Author, 2; action of advisory board, 4, 7; march from Warrenton Junction, 8-13, 76; correspondence with Burnside, 10, 11, 13, 73; correspondence with Confederates, 28; his position at Dawkins Branch, 31; time of arriving there, 52; his conduct on August 29, 50; joint order to Porter and McDowell, 52, 65, 78; Pope's order of 4:30 P. M., 62; dispatches to Morell, 82-85; dispatches to McDowell, 64, 80; Pope's orders to, 76-79; effect of Rosser's ruse, 90; Morell's testimony as to orders, 115; directions to Gen. Sturgis, 118.
Prentiss, Gen. B. M., 3.
Randall, Charles, house, 45, 109, 114, 115.
Randol, Lieut. Alanson M., 63.
Reno, Gen. Jesse L., 61, 75, ·, 95.
Reynolds, Gen. John F., 20, 24, 25, 26, 27, 47, 54, 59, 60, 61, 68, 6., 7., 85, 96, 97, 98, 99; official report, 86; testimony, 100.

Ricketts, Gen. James B., 3, 19, 41, 57, 78, 81, 85.
Robertson, Gen. Beverley H., 18, 47, 90, 91, 104.
Rosser, Col. Thomas L., 20, 25, 26, 42, 52, 55, 57, 90, 106; testimony, 101.
Ruggles, Col. George D., 76-79.
Salkehatchie Swamps, 67.
Schenck, Gen. Robert C., 20, 21, 24, 26, 27, 34, 44, 47, 59, 60, 61, 97, 99; official report, 85; testimony, 97.
Schofield, Gen. John M., member of advisory board, 4, 10, 56.
Shenandoah, 73.
Sherman, Gen. William T., 10.
Sigel, Gen. Franz. 21, 75, 77, 78, 80, 85, 95, 96, 100, 117.
Slough, Gen. J. P., 3.
Smith, Gen. T. C. H., 11.
Stanley, Gen. David S., 56.
Stevens, Gen. Isaac I., 96.
Stony Ridge, 103.
Stuart, Gen. J. E. B.; near Sudley at Poe's attack, 18, 29, 89, 91, 101, 106; going to meet Longstreet, 19, 28, 89, 102, 111; gallops to Monroe Hill, 20, 90, 102, 111; same hill called Stuart's, 108; orders dust to be raised, 25, 90, 101, 106; sends word to Jackson, 27, 102; sends word to Lee and Longstreet, 87, 88; his position in front of Porter, 33, 42, 48, 69, 90, 102, 106; time he arrived on the field, 49, 91, 102, 103, 104; his official report, 89, 91.
Stuart Hill, 23, 34, 48, · 3, 94, 108.
Sturgis, Gen. Samuel D., 57; testimony, 118.
Sudley Church, 17, 29, 89, 90, 96, 101, 105, 106.
Sudley Road, 16, 17, 51, 55, 57, 64, 65, 70, 103.
Sykes, Gen. George, 50, 57, 62, 63, 81, 115.

Terry, Gen. Alfred H., member of advisory board, 4.
Thoroughfare Gap, 18, 28, 39, 93, 102, 111.
Tower, Gen. Zealous B., 57.
Trimble, Gen. I. R., 92.
Walton, Col. J. B., 87.
Warren, Gen. G. K., his map, 30, 35, 59; testimony, 32, 34, 62, 63; dispatch, 82.
Warrenton, 37, 39, 40, 41, 93.
Warrenton Junction, 8, 73, 75, 76, 93.
Warrenton Turnpike, 65, 75, 85, 91, 100, 101, 111.
Warrenton and Washington road, 33, 34, 54, 59, 60.
Wellington, Duke of, 66.
Wheeler, W. L. B., testimony, 93.
White, Major B. S., 26, 27, 29, 42; testimony, 101.
Wilcox, Gen. Cadmus M., 19, 25, 28, 42, 46, 49, 50, 87, 88; official report, 92.
Wilderness, 67.
Young's Branch, 34, 36, 37.

www.ingramcontent.com/pod-product-compliance
Lightning Source LLC
Chambersburg PA
CBHW031338160426
43196CB00007B/714